This Much I Know

BY

LEE MICHAELS CENKUS

xulon PRESS

Copyright © 2007 by Lee Michaels Cenkus

This Much I Know
by Lee Michaels Cenkus

Printed in the United States of America

ISBN 978-1-60266-551-4

All rights reserved solely by the author. The author guarantees all contents are original and do not infringe upon the legal rights of any other person or work. No part of this book may be reproduced in any form without the permission of the author. The views expressed in this book are not necessarily those of the publisher.

Unless otherwise indicated, Bible quotations are taken from the NIV, Copyright © 1996 by Zondervan Corp., and the KJV, Copyright © 1967 by Oxford University Press.

www.xulonpress.com

Table of Contents

1. Polluted Waters 11
2. Eight Toes 15
3. A Moment of Terror 17
4. Shalom 21
5. Married in Haste 27
6. Help From Beyond 31
7. The Little Lamb 35
8. He Moves the Pool 41
9. But the Doctor Said 43
10. Broadsided 47
11. Silent for a Time 51
12. No Insufficiency 57
13. The Tough Decision 61

14. The Quiet Voice 65
15. Peril on a Summer's Night 71
16. Fountain in Hawaii 75
17. A Dynamic Finish 81
18. Without a Song 85
19. But He Could Leave 89
20. Absolutely Lost 93
21. To the Journey's End 97
22. All That Is Mine 103
23. Yet Another Opportunity 105
24. It Makes No Never Mind 113
25. New Country 117
26. Forty-Two Years Later 121
27. Family, the First Thing 127
28. The Gift of His Choosing 131
29. Together by His Design 135

Thanks

I'd like to thank the more than twenty women who openly shared their stories with me and now with you, and apologize if inadvertently in any way I have changed any detail of your story. I've striven to keep your experiences as shared with me true to your telling, both in word and spirit, but take full responsibility for their presentation.

I'd also like to thank my son Brett, who took time from his busy work schedule to review and retype both the rough and final drafts. But, most especially I appreciate his kind sensitivity to feelings of this first-time author who was often overwhelmed by the whole process.

Introduction

This small volume is a compilation of twenty-nine short stories, drawn from personal interviews with women who know God in varying capacities. Its simple intent is to increase one's knowledge and understanding of His attributes, while encouraging women to go deeper with Him, both personally and experientially. Understanding He is not a respecter of persons and has acted in certain ways in other's lives should aid us in learning to be overcomers, for we overcome by the blood of the Lamb and by the power of our testimonies. The book is intended to encourage, inspire, and instruct concerning victory over many of life's common challenges.

Though none of us here on earth can plumb the depth of the heart, mind, and character of our God, as we've walked with Him personally for various periods of time, we have learned certain things about Him. Taken all together, our stories give a good, if not wholly complete, picture of who He really is—how true, kind, tender, and wise in His dealings with His children. Above all else, we see how purposefully and skillfully He leads us, intricately weaving the various threads of our individual lives into tapestries that bring glory to Him. To this end we gladly share with you our personal stories; for in spite of what we've yet to learn, this much we do know—our God is all of the following . . .

Polluted Waters

This much I know . . . Our God is not limited by natural laws.

For with God nothing shall be impossible.
—Luke 1:37 KJV

Folks who live with city water, those who have never lived off well water, probably really can't fully understand the gravity of what happened to us a few years back. A couple years after building our dream home, I went to the mailbox one noontime to find a flyer jammed in amongst the bills, personal mailings, and the catalogs. It read something to the effect that a neighborhood meeting was being called for that Thursday night at 7 PM to discuss the problem of a toxic dump site three houses down from ours. I convinced my husband that as the newer kids on the block, by way of being neighborly, we ought at least to attend this meeting, though we were confident the problem at hand didn't really affect us directly.

About twenty families gathered that Thursday evening and formed a committee to fight the cleanup of the dump site itself, a site several years in the making. All wells on both our and the connecting blocks were to be tested, and those whose wells had been compromised were to be contacted. We learned also that the town had the bigger responsibility for the site cleanup—the previous owner having sold the place, moved away, and declared bankruptcy a couple years earlier. So began several months of negotiations. Actually, the state should have cleaned the mess up, as money had been deemed for that purpose after an EPA investigation several years prior. Unfortunately as so often happens, those funds had mysteriously been used up or mislaid or something, and the fund was broke after cleaning up only a couple of other problem areas.

During the several months of negotiations, responsibility was again assessed, and the "deep pockets" sought. Fortunately for us, the Davids among the Goliaths, our committee heads had power and know-how, so they engaged competent attorneys to act on behalf of the homeowners. Still, we felt reasonably distanced from the situation until the well test results came back. Of the twenty or so wells examined, ours was the ONLY one adversely affected. Having initially joined the group only to show solidarity, never believing we had any personal vulnerability, the test results were shocking. To add to the problem, the former owners could not be held legally responsible, and the out-of-state bank that presently owned the land gave us the corporate runaround, refusing to answer phone calls or to "own" the problem. Our small town, on the other hand, which had inadvertently permitted the dumping in the first place, hadn't the monies needed to correct the situation, and to sue them was unthinkable.

After the first well test, we went on bottled water and sought our own legal counsel. They spoke of big bucks and aquifers and such until we forsook them and any idea of representing ourselves alone in a lawsuit. It was a matter of gargantuan proportion to us—way out of our league. The situation worsened with three successive water test failures, each one worse than the former. We became desperate, knowing our house was our biggest, and only, financial asset. We had anticipated selling it after three to five years to make a real estate killing, as the market was then yielding. But real estate disclosure laws had recently been changed and now required sharing all the facts about a property up front, not that we would have considered concealing the matter, so we knew we were in deep trouble. Obviously, SOMEHOW, the matter had to be rectified. Finally, one day in an impossible position, with no foreseeable hope of resolution, we did what we should have done in the beginning. We simply laid hands on the well and, with childlike faith and expectancy, asked our heavenly Father, for whom nothing is impossible, to heal our well. We did this three times, knowing if He didn't do it we were sunk. But the health department agent on a third visit to us had unwittingly spoken the very words I needed to hear to bolster my faith. She'd casually mentioned, "This is so confusing. The tests keep coming back different with no apparent reason for the worsening changes." That little word "confusion" made the David rise up big in me, as I knew confusion not to be of the Lord, but of the enemy, Satan. And I also knew he was no match for our God. Miraculously, the fourth test taken that year proved the chemical levels in the water were all suddenly, for no explicable reason, at acceptable rates, with no pollutants showing up as present. When we sold the house three years later, the water tests mandated returned fine. Our problem was a thing of the past, settled not by man's means, but settled instead by God's hand. I still today, when I recall that time and situation, am profoundly thankful for a heavenly Father who is not limited by natural laws. A thing is not what it appears on the surface to be when He's involved, and like Paul said, some things are merely "lying wonders" (2 Thessalonians 2:9).

Eight Toes

> This much I know . . . Our God is the same today as He was in yesteryear.
>
> For I am the Lord, I change not . . .
> —Malachi 3:6 KJV

What started out to be routine bunion surgery over my Thanksgiving vacation several years ago ended up to be anything but routine. The surgery was declared a success, yet I awaited healing only to find the incision site stubbornly refusing to stay healed. Upon returning to the surgeon after a few weeks, he suggested we try a couple of treatments and antibiotics, and a month later it seemed all would be well. Yet diabolically, several weeks later the infection set in again. Once again after treatment and a period of time, it appeared healing was under way and we were home free. Yet, again, a bit later, the infection reappeared, persistent and pernicious. At this point, the infectious disease specialist and two other doctors, concurring after three months of consultation, said there was nothing left to do to "save" the toes now that two were infected and osteomyalitis had set in; but I was given a three-month regime of the strongest meds known to man, by injection thru an IV port in my chest. A visiting nurse came in daily to administer the drugs, and there was a complication from the strong medication. But also during this time, a word came to me from a dear one. Mark 11:23: "Say to this mountain be thou removed and cast into the sea and be not disbelieving." Neither of us had ever approached healing this way. In the past, we'd simply prayed for the will of the Lord to be done, a biblical, but certainly more passive, approach. We hadn't realized we had authority in Christ to curse the infection and command healing to come in Jesus' name. But I was frightened enough to overcome my skepticism, believing, in spite of my disbelief, the written promise of the Word of God. With fledgling faith, born of desperation, I spoke to the mountain of infection and commanded it to move. Three months after the treatments began, they ended, with the doctor's ominous words, "We can do nothing more. The disease has spread through two toes and is going into a third. Here is a referral for a surgeon. They must be amputated immediately." Amazingly, that referral stayed in my pocketbook until several weeks later, while showering one day I chanced to look down at my feet and noticed ten healthy toes. Tell me God doesn't heal today, as in days of old. Tell me He's changed. If you dare, I'll only smile, for I know better. The truth is that He is the same yesterday, today, and tomorrow. He set me free from a deadly disease, and how can you argue with that?

A Moment of Terror

This much I know . . . Our God is merciful.

. . .I will have mercy on whom I will have mercy. . .
—Romans 9:15 KJV

*M**ercy* is defined by Christians as "God's unmerited grace," and my story is nothing more than an evidence of that love in our lives. In October 1998, our family went on a camping trip to a Connecticut campground that had a large pond nearby. My husband, myself, and our two grown sons Matt and Mark, their wives, and Matt's dog decided to spend some time by the pond. Matt had brought a bumper with him. A bumper is a cylindrical rubber object that is thrown for dogs to retrieve, and Matt was training his black lab using this device. He would throw the bumper into the center of the pond, and the dog would then swim out to get it. At least this is how things went initially. But at some point the dog became disinterested, and when Matt threw the bumper out, the dog wandered back onto land and into some bushes. Unable to get him to obey and because the bumper was costly enough to be worth retrieving, Matt decided to go get it himself. So, he took off his jacket and shoes and waded into the water. What we didn't know was that because of the time of year, the water temperature was quite low, actually dangerously so. As Matt swam out, he later said, he could feel his strength draining away; and when the dog followed him into the water and tried to get him to play with him, it was all Matt could do with his waning strength to fend off the dog and stay afloat. To make matters worse, there were grasses underwater he had to fight against getting tangled in. He told us that as he struggled to stay afloat, he envisioned the controls of an airplane panel—he'd been trained recently as a pilot—all the gauges were going slowly down.

From the shore we could tell he looked like he might be in some trouble, though we weren't 100 percent sure. Still, his brother stripped to his shorts and jumped into the chilly water to go after Matt. Mark, too, on his way out had the same sensation of weakening debilitation and knew his strength was being sapped, but continued on, reaching Matt just ten seconds or so before Matt, according to his story, simply sank beneath the water. Somehow, in just the "nick of time," Mark was able to reach Matt, fend off the dog, and carry Matt back to the land safely.

As I watched from the shore, helpless in every way except one, I began to pray. It's strange, but I prayed, "Lord, let this be to Your glory" and, of course, "Let the rescue be a success." I guess I prayed this way because I'd learned that after all our trials God brings something good to pass, and I had settled when the boys were young whose they really were. The Lord had brought me to understand that though it was my privilege to raise them, hopefully to God-honoring and God-fearing manhood, they weren't my possessions. They really belonged to God, and though we have wonderful relationships with them and their families, their lives and purposes belong first of all to Him. Still, I'm surprised I was able and said so in my prayer to give Matt back to God if that were His choice and time. But I am ever so thankful that God was merciful to spare both my sons, as both easily could have drowned in that pond. It is simply by God's mercy and sovereignty that they are here today. I've seen much good come from the near-tragedy, in answer to my prayer that October day. Of course we all tell the story of God's mercy to everyone we can, but also and not unexpectedly, Matt has a new realization of life's frailty, along with a peace about death. He says that when he was just ten seconds from sinking, he felt no fear, only a great calmness. Then, too, the boys' relationship, always good, is deeper somehow for the experience. Other relationships have a new depth also. I, too, perhaps out of gratitude, have a deeper intimacy with the Lord than ever before, as well as a certain assurance that in all life's circumstances, in the future just as in the past, we'll have the merciful hand of the Lord upon us.

Shalom

This much I know ... Our God is real and desires we be free from Satan's strongholds.

He goes before him and consumes his foes on every side. The mountains melt like wax before the Lord.
—Psalm 97:3, 5 KJV

When I would have bad nightmares as a little girl, my mother would come into my room to comfort me and to pray. Afterwards I would think a lot about Jesus, angels, and heaven. Except for those special times, though, my very early childhood was quite normal. There were seven of us in the family—four brothers, my parents, and myself—all living very simply in a four-room "cottage" in the New England countryside, where my playground was the great outdoors. In high school I began dating Peter, and we became engaged at our high school graduation. A year later we married, moved away, and a year and a half after that started our own family. Sadly, our early married years were punctuated with increasing strife and arguments, born of our differing perspectives on most every issue. Though I knew I should submit to Peter's leadership in the home and did make some honest efforts to do so, practically speaking, I was unsuccessful, "self being on the throne of my heart" and ignorant to truth as I was. If I'm honest, looking back I can see I had an "attitude." When I felt I was right about a matter, yielding sweetly to Peter was next to impossible for me. I knew nothing about what the Bible calls "dying to self" (Galatians 2:20) or choosing to value another's opinion above my own. Then, too, anger and bitterness over the constant clashes caused an increasingly widening gap between us. Fortunately, as children we had been taken to church, albeit one where religion, rather than a personal relationship with the Lord, was taught. We knew a lot of facts about God, but as yet not He Himself. Still, having attended church sporadically in the past, we decided after the children were born to make a sincere effort to attend church faithfully and to get something out of it. We needed help badly, having no answers to our personal problems, and the counseling we'd previously sought having been of limited value.

Then a defining experience occurred that changed my life. It happened this way. The fiancé of one of my brothers, with whom I had an exceptionally close relationship, was unexpectedly, violently killed in a car accident on a rainy November day—and that just six months prior to their scheduled wedding. The tragedy traumatized me; I simply couldn't handle it, had nothing within me with which to do so. I dwelt on it constantly, and it eroded my childlike faith, for I believed if there were a God He could have prevented the chain of circumstances, any one of which would have prevented her death. That He didn't do so, I reasoned, must mean He didn't really exist or care. I judged Him with my own reasoning, having no other basis upon which to judge. The end result of five months of such thinking was despair. I was in a terrible state of mind, having spiraled downward into a hopeless condition. I couldn't focus on anything, but felt as if I were falling into pure blackness, with nothing to break the fall, nothing to grab hold of for security. But in this dreadful state I did continue to cry out to God in desperation, "If You're real You must show Yourself to me with an understandable sign. It can't be just someone coming to tell me You're real. I need to see it for myself, because if You're not real, I have to find something else to help me live." Coming to the utter end of myself one day, having put the children down to nap, I sat down in a rocking chair in my living room and started to pray. In that quiet moment, the Holy Spirit took my thoughts to the crucifixion, and I was given to understand that the Lord Jesus died an untimely violent death at a young age—the same as that of my brother's fiancé. Then He took my thoughts to the upper room where the early Christians "tarried" (Acts 1:13, 14). These Christians had "lost" Jesus, and yet they had not lost their faith. They had something I didn't have. I "understood" they knew something I didn't. Immediately my living room was filled with the manifest presence of the Lord. Absolute peace fell over me, and I sat quietly in awe as He spoke from that peace—not in an audible voice but in a gentle, loving inner voice, saying these words, "You cannot understand at this time why Anne died, but I am in control." He spoke with all of His attributes, and I felt His love, His kingship, His authority. I knew instinctively He knew of my anger, but all was forgiven. I had never had an experience like this before, and it was undeniable, bringing instant healing to my tortured soul. I knew this was what I had earlier asked of Him—to show Himself as real to me. Continuing on, I sat absorbed in the moment, and He spoke again saying, "Your brother will be well . . ." And then I heard these strange words, "When was your last female cycle?" I had been so distraught over the last few months that I had not been keeping track of things like that. I went to the calendar and checked the date, only to realize I was six to eight weeks pregnant and hadn't known until that very moment. I carried that baby until the anniversary of Anne's death, when I went into labor and delivered our daughter on a rainy November night. It seemed this gift from God, born two weeks late, but right on time, gave the family new life with which to rejoice; and it further authenticated the reality of God's visitation to me.

At the moment of His visitation, knowing undeniably He was real, it was as if my feet had been planted on solid rock. I no longer was in darkness. The peace I'd felt in His presence had melted like wax all the mountains of anger and doubt I'd previously been bound by. As a result I began reading my Bible with new eyes and hungered to know truth. Shortly thereafter we were led to a church that taught the Bible as God's sure Word and as the foundation for healthy relationships and living. The importance of the former was inestimable, for if I'd simply had an experience with the Lord but not pursued Him, it would have been like meeting a man and marrying but never again speaking to him. The initial introduction and wedding would be of small consequence in the course of the entire lifetime of that relationship. I believe the devil works overtime to keep us from such personal experiences—to keep us in darkness, for our spiritual foundation comes from revelation of who He really is. It is revealed to us even as it was to Peter, in the Father's time and at His will, in personal but real ways. Subsequently, I've become a doer of the Word. I no longer just know about God, but am growing in personally knowing Him. In learning to obey His written Word, God has given me power to break the demonic strongholds once held over me. Such were my attitudes towards Peter, the strife and incorrect thinking about physical marital lovemaking. At one point in my childhood I had been sexually abused, and the memories of those experiences had taken my thoughts captive. Like unwanted guests, they continued to show up periodically whenever they chose. The healing in this area has been a long, gradual process.

Many people believe in angels but not demon beings, though both are real and need to be understood to have a proper biblical perspective. God has not given us the spirit of fear, nor of anger, nor discord. Anything that we do not have control over has control over us and needs to be dealt with—put to death—be it the fruit of the flesh or demonic activity. Yielding to it only increases its power over us. Sometimes we inherit tendencies and generational iniquities. I had many such issues and insecurities, but then we all struggle with such, and so ought not be ashamed to admit it is so. Some folks mistakenly believe all is fine in their families and do not recognize there's a spirit of pride and self-righteousness there. Simply stated, I was now learning all that our salvation entails—exactly what Jesus bought for us on the cross by His shed blood. The very word salvation, as I understand it, includes within it eternal security, health, and healing of damaged emotions. Everything He did for us on the cross is ours if we will appropriate it. Jesus' death gives us authority over the flesh and the demonic, hence the ability to have victory and freedom from bondage and mental strongholds, such as were strangling me. Prior to coming to this new scriptural understanding, I had not recognized my part in the marital strife, for I saw myself merely as a victim, having had certain acts perpetrated upon me as a child. What I had failed to realize was my responsibility in choosing subsequently to maintain anger, bitterness, and unforgiveness, eventually opening the door to extreme hatred by transferring those negatives from my abuser to my husband. I learned it was imperative I be brutally honest with myself and God in calling my behavior what He does—sin—and in renouncing it. It was helpful to learn that most perpetrators were once innocent children themselves, who had become victims of other sinful choices. Also, I learned that if terrible things happened to me, a greater grace is available to enable me to forgive and be free from their grip, IF I'll just agree with God. (And if I want to and if I will appropriate His healing thoughts, Scriptures, and behaviors.) I had to give up self-justification if I wanted this grace and have total truth in my innermost parts. God does not play games. He is deadly serious about our healing, but also He will not do that part of healing that is ours to do. We must choose to embrace the truth, to obey Him in it, regardless of its making sense or the number of times we need to go back to them and the process again and again, until He brings the full measure of it to bear in His time. This does not often result in overnight release, but in delay God is strengthening our relationship with Him, teaching us to abide and to be established in biblical mindsets, forsaking and replacing the old rotten thinking with the rock of His truth.

It took years for me to overcome the marital intimacy problem. I had to continually pray, choosing life, not death, in our relationship. Peter also in this time was changing, growing much in patience, and learning to recognize the difference between lust and real love for me. For he, like all of us today to greater and lesser degrees, was tainted with the images on television, in commercials, and in magazines. These images glorify lust and do not teach the truth that lust is really nothing more than self-gratification, while love seeks to serve the beloved, and primarily gives pleasure to another for his or her sake alone. We fail to see lust as she is—marital intimacy's great enemy, and that it must be renounced, forsaken, and its avenues avoided.

To sum things up, I'd just say that the rock foundation of biblical truths learned and obeyed brought Peter and me release and healing. But release and healing, again, are only actuated to the degree that our personal relationships with the Lord are vital and continue to grow. I cannot thank Him enough that when we seek Him in reality and experience, He himself answers our call and comes to us that we might ultimately live to His glory, free from bondage and full of thanksgiving.

Married in Haste

This much I know . . . A part of really knowing God requires embracing suffering, but in that suffering He is present in an ever-deepening way.

For this is thankworthy if a man for conscience toward God endure grief, suffering wrongfully. For what glory is it, if, when ye be buffeted for your faults, ye shall take it patiently? but if, when ye do well, and suffer for it, ye take it patiently, this is acceptable with God.
— 1 Peter 2:19, 20 KJV

All my life I've been a runner, running from difficult situations rather than facing problems squarely and working them through to good conclusions. It was just easier for me to run than persevere when life was hard and hurtful. But I'm learning now that escape is not the answer to my difficulties, for if I don't confront them I'm not going to gain anything in the long run. Instead, I only compound the problems by trading one issue for another as they all pile up, one atop another. They follow me, for in their essence they are really more internal than external and can't be simply shed like unwanted garments.

As a child I was quiet, shy, introverted. I didn't like people very much. Actually, I hated childhood and have never wanted to go back there. Experience taught me early on that people were hurtful. Really it wasn't until college that I began to reach out to folks and began making attempts to become friendly.

Backtracking, when I was about seven years old, I did attend a lovely community church and greatly enjoyed that experience. It was a warm place to be, with music and guitar players, and I remember wanting to be a "saint," though I didn't have a clue how to become such. But then we moved from Massachusetts to Connecticut, and in the process stopped going to church, so that good thing ceased to influence and encourage me.

My heart's lifelong desire has always been just to be married. It seemed my whole existence and happiness depended upon it. Sadly, though, in that pursuit, I had many failed relationships. Even now, years later, I have regrets for the things I did that I wish I hadn't done while pursuing that goal. I was always looking for an ideal, wanting love and commitment but not going about it the right way. So, at the age of twenty-nine, after breaking off a three-year relationship that I'd thought would lead to marriage, I forsook my long-cherished dream. I returned home disillusioned, deciding not to be involved with anyone again. I simply gave up. I figured I wasn't qualified to have a marital relationship. Surprisingly, I grew to be happy nonetheless, living at home with my parents and grandmother. That small world was very satisfying, but three months into it my mother and sister thought I should resume dating. I had never really wanted to date, never enjoyed that process. Getting to know new people wasn't fun for me, and, besides, I tended to fall into love too easily and get serious too quickly. But I guess to appease them I let them talk me into a date with Sam.

We drove that first night into New York City, which was extraordinary in one way. Previously, I'd had this quirky problem—trouble riding passenger in a car, falling asleep and then waking up confused and angry. But Sam was a great driver, and, for the first time, I enjoyed the uneventful ride to and from the city with none of the regular problems. We spent the time in the city bar-hopping, which wasn't me at all. I had caffeine withdrawal, and my feet hurt from new shoes. I didn't believe Sam was even interested in me, because all he talked about all night was his past girlfriends. Yet, at the evening's end, he asked me to go with him to a Bible study. Honestly, I thought him a hypocrite, but I said yes anyway. I did stipulate that on our second date we had to have a chaperone, since the date was to be a meal alone at his house before the study. As it happened, the chaperone cancelled at the last minute but encouraged me to go anyway. Sam made a wonderful duck dinner. I was impressed with his culinary skills and the Bible study that followed. My joke ever since has been I was looking for a husband (once again), but what I really found was God.

I did think Sam was cute, and our relationship developed quickly. Soon after that we married and almost immediately began to have marital difficulties. We are exact opposites, and while there was much I truly admired about him, there were some things I discovered that looked different after marriage from the way they had before. These became huge areas of frustration, and I became aware I was still trying to grasp at love, "to feel love," and couldn't quite get my hands on the reality as I deemed it. Worse yet, I couldn't just run away now. I'd taken a vow, and there would still be me to deal with. I recognized it wasn't just Sam's issues that were the problem, but mine as well. For a long time I felt with Sam that if I just submitted more, or did things "just right," I'd get the love I craved. So my submission was really a veiled attempt to manipulate him and the hand of God. Also, it wasn't really true submission, which is to yield to suffering, if necessary, with sweetness, simply because it's the God-honoring, right thing to do. That's where I am right now—accepting I may never get the love and companionship I desire from Sam, but letting that be okay. We're at a very low time, truthfully. He's often emotionally absent though we're always in each other's company. There's no physical contact, by his choice, and only the most basic verbal communication. I realize now that it's not my being a perfect wife that will change things. I've had a lot of guilt about my past that impels me to do this thing right, as if to make up for those poor choices and failures. The truth is, though, it's a mistake to believe that because I'm a Christian, if I do it all right, as the books imply, then I'll get a set, desired result. I've learned from older, believing wives that which I need to understand, that in suffering, even suffering in marriage, I am pressed in deeper to the Lord, the One who truly meets my needs. No man can fulfill me completely ultimately, even if he were to try. That makes me see how very precious all the Lord's thoughts are toward me. And then, too, I recognize how little I really love Sam, when I compare God's love for me to mine for Sam. When I can stop focusing so much on what I'm not getting and instead look to the Lord and love on Him, then I can draw from that love to give to my husband; and it's okay. I did make a vow when I married and will stay in this marriage, if only because it honors and pleases the Lord. I'm growing in wanting to please Him more than in wanting to have my own way. Now I pray not that my husband will change in his personal idiosyncrasies so much as that he will grow to have a healthy, deepening relationship with God also. And I'm seeing answered prayer as he desires new friendships with men at church and is learning more about interpersonal relationships. Still, some days are harder than others, if I'm honest, as the old ways and thought patterns die hard. But I am finding His peace and presence a great compensation for the occasional suffering that used to be unbearable.

Help From Beyond

> This much I know . . . Our God cares for us by sending angels when we need special help.

> Are not all angels ministering spirits sent to serve those who will inherit salvation?
> —Hebrews 1:14 NIV

There's a lot of nonsense popular today about angels. They're a trendy conversation topic—even to the point of becoming a cult-like thing. We see their representations on store shelves everywhere—some tasteful, some outlandish, some "gee-gawish." This being the case, I almost hesitate to share their presence in my life, but I can't escape the part they have played, as by His commands they have kept me safe, assisted and guided me several times, and given me much peace overall. I'm increasingly aware of their ministry and thankful for their presence. My understanding of the biblical truth about angels is that each one of us has at least one assigned to us from childhood, probably throughout life, and upon our death, he will escort us into the presence of Jesus. Alongside the Holy Spirit, they are dispatched by God so we are not alone in difficult circumstances where human help would fail us. They can be conduits of comfort, healing, peace, and are warriors against evil. They are a gift from the Father and known to us strictly by spiritual perception. By that I mean, though, they may minister unaware, and no doubt do so, as we are aware of their presence only through the power of the Holy Spirit and sometimes only after the fact.

Attention is not so much to be given to them, but rather to God, whom both they and we, as created beings, serve together, though in differing dimensions. They can communicate with us and are sensitive to offending God. The Bible speaks of our not taking their admonitions lightly. One note here is worthy of mention. Because there also exist "angels of darkness" who mask themselves as "spirits of light," we must use discernment in angels' presence (Galatians 1:8). If they dishonor God or do not bring His peace, violate His ways or His scriptures, we should reject their inspiration. My personal experiences with angels over the years, though very real, have not necessarily been earth shaking. Nonetheless, even in their simplicity, they have been meaningful and continuous. The following are a few examples.

One time I ordered a bedspread from a catalog supplier and had gone to the mall to pick it up. Upon receiving it, I kept sensing an insistence I open the package, but did not at first, instead proceeding directly back to my car. I started driving home but finally had to yield, pulling the car over and opening the package to discover the wrong spread. Small as this example is, it pointed up to me the need to "listen" to the inner impression that angels can, along with the Holy Spirit, give. In that case, the reason was just to save me wasted time and teach me to "listen" with an ear to hear.

Another time on one of the coldest days of the winter here in Connecticut, when the weatherman was advising folks not to be outdoors unless they absolutely needed to be, and to bring all pets indoors because of the frigid temps, I nevertheless chose to go shopping for a necessary item. My car, not being new, began to do something funny that day; it would not accelerate when I depressed the gas pedal. Once upon the way, with the car acting up, I became afraid to even get off the highway. This was in the days before cell phones, and I was afraid I'd get stranded on some out-of-highway road and get hypothermia while waiting for help. My plan was just to stay on the far right-hand side of the highway, which I did until I exited at the shopping center, did what I needed to do and returned home safely. I prayed all the while for divine help. Later that same day my son took the car around the corner, got stuck, and had to be rescued.

In another incident, my car simply died in a parking lot where there were no phones. Just as I was asking God for help, a tow truck appeared from nowhere and stopped near me. I quickly ran to it and told the driver, "I don't know why you're here, but after you take care of whatever you came for would you please help me?" He answered, "I was just given the thought I should get some dog food. I'm not here for any other reason, so I'll be happy to help." And he did.

In yet another instance we were on a trip to Africa, on a puddle jumper plane going somewhere. Typically, I ask the Lord when I fly to send His angels to guide and be with my plane. It just so happened that day that, as we were descending, one of the plane's tires blew out. Everyone was understandably frightened, but in spite of the problem we had a textbook smooth landing, as if the plane were being set down gently by unseen hands.

Finally, there was the time, while at a faith-sharing group at church, the subject of angels came up. I shared my beliefs with several women, but was met with blank stares, as if to say, "Oh yeah, we all believed that stuff when we were young, but now we're mature and know better." I returned home feeling guilty I'd communicated God's truth so poorly and actually apologized to Him. The following week I returned to the group to hear their amazing stories. One lady shared that a friend had a second friend literally on her deathbed in a hospital, awaiting the arrival of all her eight children so she could say her final good-byes. She slipped into a coma. The hospital staff, with all their medical knowledge, didn't believe she'd live until evening. Lady #1 had on an angel pin, took it off and pinned it on the dying mother's Johnny coat, praying as she did so. The comatose woman not only lingered until the eight children arrived, but when all were assembled round her bed, awoke from the coma to speak to each one last time.

Another woman told me her son in the military was stationed in Saudi Arabia during Desert Storm. She had not heard from him in quite some time and was very worried, so she requested in prayer that God send an angel to speak to him and tell him to call home. That very night she received a phone call saying he was alright, laying her fears to rest. Still another lady told me that last week while walking on the sidewalk, she'd tripped; and her legs went right out behind her in such a way she should have gone splat, yet "somehow" her legs got back under her body. She thought she might well have been caught by an unseen helper and set aright. I guess the upshot of all the ladies' telling their stories is that, in sharing about angels being one of God's good gifts to us, others became aware of their presence. So while it may be we aren't always aware of them and their ministries to us, it is nevertheless also true that a heightened awareness of their existence and purpose can at other times not only strengthen us, but also produce encouragement for others on their pilgrim paths.

The Little Lamb

> This much I know . . . Our God is the good shepherd. He leads His sheep along desired paths for His name's sake.
> The Lord is my shepherd . . .
> —Psalm 23:1 KJV

There's a book entitled *A Shepherd Looks at His Sheep* by Phillip Keller that several of us recently used in a small neighborhood Bible study. It occurs to me that the way in which the shepherd in that little volume cares for his sheep is exactly the way the Lord has always taken care of me, His little lamb.

As a baby He placed me right into "green pastures," into the home of two strong, but gentle, loving, healthy Christian believers, who took all of us children to church regularly, but, more importantly, modeled Christlikeness before us. Early on, and no doubt due to those influences, I found myself ofttimes besides "still waters," Him restoring my soul. One place this happened, oddly enough, was at the dentist's office. The dentist in my day was a formidable foe. Without modern instruments, technology, or the anesthetics available today, a visit to the dentist most assuredly involved pain, sometimes much pain if a nerve were involved in the chosen procedure. I clearly remember being frightened as I'd await my turn in "the chair" and more than once fled to safety in the basement of the building, where I'd frantically repeat the twenty-third Psalm to myself until His Spirit quieted mine enough to return upstairs to be worked on.

Also no doubt due to the early influences of both church and home, in my teen years I would seek the fellowship of other believers rather than the companionship of the world. In my middle teen years, the Shepherd brought me into contact with a group of young committed Catholic girls who challenged me in my faith. I was later to understand this to be a providential leading, as my future husband attended that particular church, and it evolved that if we were to marry and worship together, which we desired to do, it would be in his church home, for he was firm in this choice. It was no problem for me, though, because just a little while before meeting Ben, the Shepherd had led me to the San Francisco Cow Palace to a Billy Graham Crusade, where by a heartfelt and life-changing decision, I'd begun a personal relationship with Jesus Christ and given Him the lordship of my life. Thus secure in His salvation, being in His "forever" family, plus having the prior influence of the godly girls in my high school years, the place of worship was not of such importance as to be a stumbling block to our marrying.

Wolves and strange doctrines can attack young lambs if the Shepherd does not guard them as He leads them along to new grasslands. They'd be easy prey from predators, apart from His presence and protection, and so He guarded my heart and mind by teaching me scriptural truths and wisdom from the Bible. One memorable example of this divine understanding involved our second son and a particular childhood challenge.

Willie was a delightful little guy and lots of fun until he entered a difficult period in the third grade. At that point he began having trouble focusing on his schoolwork and slipped into the role of class clown. While the teacher was at the board instructing, he'd tune out instead of listening, occupying himself drawing pictures of military tanks and such as interested him. Consequently, he began to fail in his schoolwork, and the failure affected his self-esteem. Anger surfaced as a direct result, and hurt exploded into fights on the school playground. We were called into the office repeatedly. At our wits' end as to how to deal with the problem, and understanding its very serious consequences if left unresolved, I cried out to the Lord; and He led me from the high craggy place of frustration and confusion to a sweet level grassy land of safety and peace. He led me to understand what Willie was good at and enjoyed. Break dancing being his prime interest at that time, we encouraged him in that after-school activity. The many hours he spent perfecting the art form had a positive effect on him. He began to evidence a new confidence, performing better in class and eventually becoming an excellent athlete. Ultimately he gained access to a military academy from which he was graduated into Special Forces, where he actively serves today.

We moved from potential failure to lifetime success because of God's leading us to incite and later plan for Willie's life. But the leading and protection of God's sheep is always dependent upon the sheep's willingness to stay near enough the Shepherd to hear His voice of guidance and warning. To be led to such pastures as fulfill God's purposes requires humility. If we aren't careful, it's easy to see ourselves as the world sees us, self-sufficient and exalted, and not to understand the truth that He is the one who gives us the ability to achieve anything good. He is our source, not we ourselves, and pride can blind us from seeing our need for a Shepherd.

In the past few years, I've had blurriness in my eyes that has caused me to fear, or said another way, to be on high cliffs of undue concern, where I've had no choice but to cling to the shepherd. Once for a long period of recuperation after eye surgery, until my visual clarity returned, everything I viewed appeared fuzzy. As I slowly healed, I had an interesting experience one morning while gazing out the window at the ocean. My entire morning's view was misted, obscured by cloudiness. Yet strangely, hours later, sitting still at that same spot, gazing out the same window at the same ocean view, but the fog now lifted, I could see clearly for miles.

It is said sheep can't drink from rushing waters but instead are refreshed from quiet streams. So we need to be willing to sit quietly and sometimes for a lengthy period of time before the Lord, awaiting His lifting of the fog in our lives and allowing Him to bring us again to clear not brackish waters, the truth not fuzzy but fully comprehensible. Strangely, another high place of danger is that of low self-esteem. From this place one is preoccupied primarily with the self and its deficiencies. I know for many years I cared tremendously about my "packaging," concealing protruding teeth and big ears, putting undue emphasis on just the right color of hair and clothing style. While all of these concerns do have a legitimate place in our lives, they became precipices in mine when they became issues of such great importance. Learning to accept myself and to see myself through God's eyes has been a journey.

One grey winter's day, while having my quiet time with the Lord, He made me aware of a certain scene—endless rows of barren trees, stripped of all flowers and leaves. All I saw were spindly tree trunks, split bark, and odd knobs jutting out all over them. Yet oddly, there was beauty in their essence, and I understand that's how the Shepherd sees me. My packaging is of little to no great worth to Him. It's my inner self—my soul—He loves and nourishes, and I must struggle sometimes still to agree with Him—to value what He does in me and have a quiet thankful acceptance of His creation, instead of being unsettled by all my perceived beauty flaws.

As I look back over the past sixty years of my life, I have the advantage of viewing the Shepherd's work in my life more or less as a whole. Now I see that in my early years, He allowed me to frolic in pastures partly of my own choosing; yet His sheep dogs of truth and wisdom kept me from straying too far from Him. In my latter years, I see how He continues to keep me close to His side, that I might have the security of His presence in all the upcoming challenges of aging and watching life's journey come to its end in many I know and love. But above all, I see now as King David once saw that the lines have fallen for me in pleasant places, and goodness and mercy have followed me all the days of my life. Surely then after all is said and done, I shall dwell in the house of the Lord forever.

He Moves the Pool

This much I know . . . Our God is compassionate, stooping to care for even the mundane things that concern His children.

. . . the Lord's . . . compassions fail not.
—Lamentations 3:22, 23 KJV

For many years, I found one of my life's most difficult challenges was summer vacation. With three kids, five years apart in age chronologically but eight or more years developmentally, and having a limited income with very little in discretionary funds, I came to literally despise the endless weeks of summer, during which I desperately tried to keep the kids fruitfully occupied. Apart from two weeks at the family place and later two weeks at a camping facility, the remainder of the long hot days were mine alone to fill. So when our immediate neighbors, whose property line conjoined ours in a triangular configuration, one day began cutting down all the trees bordering our common yard and overlooking our porch room, I became upset. My husband inquired of them, only to discover they intended to put in an in-ground swimming pool in the opened area.

The knowledge hit me hard, as I could not imagine them splashing about merrily as the kids and I sat and listened from the sunroom/porch. While I did not covet their good fortune to have the pool, I simply felt it was too much for us to be so tempted, watching their aquatic fun from dry land so near. So I told my husband that if God could open the Red sea for His Israelite children, then surely in compassion for me, He could move the swimming pool to the other side of their property, out of our eyeshot and ear range. Wyatt laughed and said it was impossible—that their leeching fields were on the other side of their yard. But faith rose up big in me for the first time, and I believed regardless. Several days passed until a time came when, while driving in our common driveway, I noticed trees being taken down now on the right side of the neighbors' home. I immediately called Wyatt to tell him the news—my miracle was happening, but he only laughed and reiterated it couldn't be. But later that evening after dinner, to humor me, he wandered next door to ask about the fresh tree cutting, and to his amazement, these were our neighbor's words, "It's the darndest thing; we just don't understand it. But apparently the plot plans filed at the town hall must have been wrong, for the leeching fields are on the left side after all." Of course I knew better! And though it was the first time God did the impossible to show his compassion for me, it was to be far from the last.

But the Doctor Said

This much I know . . . Our God is a healer.

> But unto you that fear my name shall the Sun of righteousness arise with healing in his wings . . .
> —Malachi 4:2 KJV

Until I was fifty-five, I enjoyed wonderful health, except for the occasional cold and less occasional flu. I believed I'd never face serious illness and had walked in that confidence all my life. Then one September noontime, while lunching at an inn in the Poconos, out of nowhere, I began feeling a strange sensation in my right forearm. It was as if something were vaporizing, turning to liquid under my skin, and my fingers began tingling. The phenomena continued for a couple of weeks, so I made a doctor's appointment, though I somehow already knew what was wrong. Tests and a brain scan confirmed my dark suspicions—the diagnosis. MS demylenation showed up in the scan, and the top notch, big city neurologist confirmed with words what I dreaded to hear. But his report was not to be the final one, because God had me by now traveling down an entirely new road—one I'd only heard about before—one where what one sees, feels, and hears is at the mercy of what God says. Put another way, the reality of a situation must yield to truth as His word proclaims it.

Firstly He strengthened my heart, giving it the ability to hold fast to a scripture promise in the book of Hebrews—the one that tells us that against all hope Abraham believed—staggering not at the promise, but calling into being that which was not (Romans 4:17, 20). For Abraham that was an heir, a son of his own issue, from his and Sarah's more than eighty-year-old bodies. For me it would mean speaking health and life into a diseased limb.

Secondly, later in the fall, while practicing His presence (spending time sitting alone with Him, talking over my feelings and problem, and then quietly worshipping Him and listening for His response), He spoke a personal or *rhema* word, in which He promised healing if I'd walk steadily with Him. I wrote down the word, time, and date to refer back to often when my faith grew weak. Yet despite His word, the symptoms persisted, annoying at first, confusing at times, but mostly scary as they continued to increase in intensity and duration. One evening episode even resulted in brief temporary paralysis. Then in late October, when faith and doubt collided, I sought the Lord earnestly "just one more time" to settle the matter. Was it really His voice I'd heard that September afternoon, or merely my own—so deeply desiring healing that I'd conjured up the words I wanted to hear.

With childlike humility, I asked the Lord to confirm His word and promised afterwards it would be settled. Three times that day, on a radio broadcast, on a television show, and in a closing prayer at a small neighborhood Bible study, someone said these precious words, "Whose report will you believe?" And I knew I had my answer. I would believe God's report, not the doctor's, nor the very real report of my troubled body. The matter established, I would cling to

God's promise to me, believing my present reality would ultimately have to yield to the truth of God's Word and line up with that.

For approximately one to two months following that date, nothing definitively changed, but at about the three-month mark, my healing slowly began to materialize. And for the last five and a half years, I've been just fine, enjoying good health and the energy to do all He calls me to. Some say it's remission, but I know better. I care not a whit that others don't understand. I only sorrow that they know Him not in this capacity, as Jehovah Rophi, the god who heals . . . the same yesterday, today, and tomorrow, no respecter of persons and not bound by natural laws, doctors' prognoses, or other "realities."

As they say, "One with an experience with the true God is never at the mercy of one with a mere doctrine." Jesus is a healer today, just as He was in the days He walked the earth, and I'm just one of multitudes who've experienced that goodness. The means He used, uses, is of no account, for He is never limited, and He alone chooses the pathway of healing that pleases Him and suits His purposes. For me that meant applying the written Word to my body, much as if it were medicine, and then resting in His promise until the healing manifested fully.

Broadsided

> This much I know . . . Our God is the one who brings us victoriously through the trials of life.

> For the LORD God is a sun and shield: the LORD will give grace and glory: no good thing will he withhold from them that walk uprightly.
> —Psalm 84:11 KJV

I was just like Much-Afraid in Hannah Hurnard's *Hinds' Feet on High Places* in 1986. A tired, pressed in on all sides, thirty-five-year-old mother of a six-year-old daughter and newborn Down syndrome son, I awoke one morning to my husband's announcement that he had never loved me and was leaving us. All security was suddenly, terrifyingly ripped from my life in a day, and I faced the unthinkable, aloneness and divorce. Deserted, troubled in mind, and physically exhausted, I despaired. I had no resources to fall back upon—no in-state family—no job—and, worst of all, no means of respite from the daily duties that motherhood and single parenting required. Thoughts of the future sent me into a tailspin, so fearful was I. Honestly, much like Hagar, cast out and alone, except for my children, death looked a welcome relief. But also, just as Hagar did, I cried out to a God I didn't know well, and He heard, as He always does, my desperate cries, coming eventually to be my sun and shield.

To protect my mind from its endless tortuous negative self talk, He brought me immediately to a woman, who introduced me to a church that would teach me the truths that would wash over my thoughts and mind. It was there in that church I discovered Jesus as personal Savior, and in His grace He lavished mentors and new friends on my very quickly. Those dear folks walked me through countless dark days and long teary nights, when I kept hoping against hope my husband would have a change of heart and return to us.

Jesus Himself, in my suffering, became my consolation, and He began to provide financially for me as well—first in a home sewing business, with so many clients I had to turn some away. Then He provided short runaway weekends and vacations for refreshment, and restrengthening, love gifts of money, unexpected and perfectly timed to meet critical needs. But His best gift after Himself was the people, brothers and sisters in the Lord, who gave themselves to us generously day and night. Many encouraged me "to go deeper" with the Lord, to develop a lifelong relationship built on quiet trust of Him alone. The Bible, Christian books, and such became my constant companions, as well as "of the flesh" prayer partners and small groups of like-minded believers.

The Lord Himself, as He promised, now became, in tangible ways, my Provider, my Deliver, and my Husband, absolutely essential to my well-being, because in my rejection I desperately craved love and marriage. In the next eleven years, this desire to be remarried was sorely tested, as I took part in seventeen weddings—having to learn in each to crucify my own desires and to enter unfeignedly into others' joy. But skillfully He led me, much like Much-

Afraid, through sorrows, delayed promises, and uncertainties to know revealed secrets and to walk in high places.

One specific truth He impressed upon me was the need and joy of "giving"—either myself in some way or from my meager storehouse. No matter how small the gift, blessing others became my survival mode, and then my strength, and finally the channel of my own provision, as the law of recompense kicked in. When I gave, I received back; and God revealed again and again He is a God of grace and glory, showering kindness and goodness upon this child.

Among the countless blessings returned to me were my son's learning to swim, bowl, and eventually becoming a Special Olympics contender. My daughter successfully navigated childhood and the particularly difficult teen and high school years to later enter full-time Christian service. Not withholding any good thing, in the fullness of time, eight years ago, after an eleven-year wait, the Lord brought me the desire of my heart . . . a Christian husband.

From my vantage point today, I can see how God used those difficult but necessary eleven years to take me from the broken, frightened, helpless woman I was to the confident overcomer (in Him) I am today. Now I'm certain in the knowledge that our God will bring His kids victoriously through life's darker seasons if we will but cooperate with Him and not give in to despair. He is ever full of grace and, in meeting all my needs, continued to bring glory to Himself, as His excellent character was and is today revealed in His endless kindness, faithfulness, and love.

Silent for a Time

This much I know . . . Our God is a redeemer.

He shall be silent in His love.
— Zephaniah 3:17 KJV

God went out to redeem a people for Himself, and to make a name for Himself, to perform great and awesome works.
—2 Samuel 7:23 KJV

My life has never been easy. When I was quite young, my older twin brothers, then in their late teens, both developed schizophrenia. This affected my life big time, because my parents, from that time on, took on their issues and care as their sole preoccupation. Mom and Dad's lives narrowed in scope with each passing year, for the boys continued to grow worse as they aged; so being the only normal functioning sibling, it has befallen to me increasingly to care for my parents as they've aged. Today they both are in their eighties and have cancer and other physical ailments that keep them housebound. They no longer drive, cook very little, and are virtually dependent upon me to take them to their respective doctor appointments, to do their shopping, and daily to visit my brothers who are presently institutionalized in different towns.

But in spite of all that's on my plate, I'm not complaining, for God has been my constant companion and source of strength for years now. Typically, I start my mornings with Him in song and Bible reading and continue to check in with Him throughout the day. Still, it emotionally moves me to remember a time I'd never thought would come, but during which two of God's characteristics came to have very special significance for me.

The circumstances of that time were as follows. Sandra, our twenty-year-old daughter, then a third-year college student, in a phone call one evening admitted to us that she was pregnant. Fearing this could happen, and having prayed mightily against it, I was shocked and confounded at God's allowing it to be so. I truly believed my concern, fervent prayers, and faithful service for Him would have prevented this happening. Then too, shame kept me from sharing the terrible news with others, so I was isolated for months in my misery.

Sandra, on the other hand, always a take-charge, "I can do it if I stick to it" sort of girl, despite the hurdles from early on, was determined to finish her last undergraduate year of study and keep the baby as well. We wholeheartedly supported those choices, especially keeping the baby, as we know children are a gift from God, no matter the circumstance of their conception. But the college she attended was out of state, a two-hour drive from us, a distance that prohibited our being on-site to help in the daily necessary ways; and both my I and my husband worked, precluding our watching the baby in our home, even if Sandra would have let us have her. Then, too, there was another daunting practical concern. Sandra was on partial scholarship and had only a summer waitressing job to provide for herself financially; nevertheless, she was resolved to have her baby by her side, finish school, and do whatever it took to meet her career goals.

As the pregnancy progressed, I tried a number of things to find a resolution to her housing and childcare problems, including calling churches in her college area to see if they knew of anyone who could help. But despite my efforts and mountains of prayer, God was silent for months. I did not then know the Zephaniah scripture that speaks of His being silent in love, so His silence was something new and confusing to me. It seemed as if He were almost uncaring, and while I knew intellectually that His delays are not necessarily denials, as the weeks dragged on and the pregnancy progressed, I became more and more anxious. No doors readily opened, and, for all my head knowledge about God's love, I felt abandoned, until the fullness of time. That is, the time He chooses to intervene in the situation, and we see His hand moving on our behalf.

The solution to our dilemma, when it came, amazed even me. Unbeknownst to us, a young Catholic couple that lived near Sandra's college had been prayerfully seeking the Lord to bring to them a young pregnant woman needing assistance, to whom they might show His love. Their hearts were tender towards that ministry, as they saw children as God's reward, a blessing, not a curse. They were mindful of the current culture's twisted thinking, which views children as a burden, an accident, an impediment to one's personal fulfillment. Amy and Mark themselves had a young son at the time, very limited resources, and only two small extra rooms in their home that Sandra could use, but they didn't let what they lacked become a consideration in their decision.

What they did have was hearts of love for the Lord and Sandra and Lauren, Sandra's daughter, wisdom, and an old-fashioned simple lifestyle they were willing to share. And because they didn't spend time on television, movies, expensive programs at the gym, or other worldly entertainments, they were personally available to Sandra at any given time to help with Lauren, no small blessing. Amy watched the babies while Sandra was in classes, and when Sandra was home, Amy modeled Christlike motherhood to her. Sandra saw patience, kindness, gentleness, and love, as well as a highly functional marriage dynamic when Mark was at home. Both Amy and Mark gave of themselves, their time, and their meager resources sacrificially.

Quite frankly, as I watched God redeem our sad situation, make something good out of what had initially looked to be such a mess, I was overwhelmed at His goodness to Sandra. It is true that, upon discovering the pregnancy, she had asked God for His forgiveness and thereby positioned herself for Him to act on her behalf; but that He so beautifully orchestrated things as He did caused even my heart to rejoice. No doubt any one of a number of women ultimately might have stepped up to the plate to take Sandra and Lauren in, but God arranged it to be exactly the type believer my daughter would respect and want to emulate, therein being open to learn life skills from. Sandra herself had always been a thinker, and to be given a model whose brain she could pick, who was what Elisabeth Elliott would term a "deep well," was perfection itself.

Then, too, Amy and Mark's lifestyle, that they were content of an evening to simply walk the baby to the park or peruse the public library shelves for a good book, was both arresting and pivotal for Sandra. She watched firsthand lives stripped of most twentieth-century trappings, yet saw real contentment and purpose there. The shallow values her generation as a whole held were no match for the godly virtues modeled before her. The year Sandra spent in Amy and Mark's house was life changing and probably more foundational than her entire four years of college academic instruction. To this day, Sandra keeps in touch with them, and actually Amy was an honored guest at Sandra's wedding a short while ago.

Of a truth, a mother's heart can never be at rest if her children's lives are in shipwreck and their hearts sorrowing. That's where I was back then when Sandra's unplanned pregnancy took over our lives. But in that awful silent time, in God's waiting room, I realize now, far from being uncaring, He was instead working out a miracle solution to the mess we'd gotten ourselves into. Looking back with some distance, I see that awful time differently now. Above all, I see how God used it to teach me things about Himself I wouldn't have known otherwise. So if I had it to do again, would I want it to be different? Not really—to know my God is a redeemer not only of souls, but also of situations is wonderful knowledge to have.

Well, that's my story, except to say that I've done it both ways over the years—kept control of a messy situation, trying to work it out myself, and given it over to the Lord, and there's no comparison. My way was always a hit or miss thing—but His always ultimately involved a redemptive miracle worked out over time that brought about good for all concerned.

No Insufficiency

> This much I know . . . Our God is sufficient for every need.
>
> Not that we are sufficient of ourselves to think any thing as of ourselves; but our sufficiency is of God.
> —2 Corinthians 3:5 KJV

Unfortunately, my parents' marriage wasn't a happy one. My dad was an Irish policeman, given to drink and abuse. My mother often told me that the only joy and stabilizing factor in her life was her children, my brother and me, both adopted in infancy. She impressed upon me early on that I was chosen, beloved, and had three mothers—a birth mom, herself, and the Holy Mother Mary. Because of this knowledge, I grew up happy, despite the problematic environment in our home.

My mother had her own in-home beauty shop, so I learned at her side, quite young, both homemaking and business skills. Because she praised me in these, I grew to feel good about myself. I married Ralph young, and we quickly added two sons to our new family. In the early years of marriage, we did most everything together, enjoying life's simple pleasures, nature, games, and outings. To my thinking "all our dories were hunky." I was certainly content, if not a bit naïve, so when Ralph, around the seven-year marriage mark, changed his focus from us to other things, first running in marathons, then to a local coffee house, I was caught off guard. He's different from me anyway—as is often the case with husbands and wives. I'm sort of easygoing, contented, and primarily family-oriented. He's more restless by nature, outward, needing to change his focus periodically, and sells out almost obsessively to whatever his new interest is.

That's exactly what I thought was happening those many years ago. I never in my wildest imagination considered betrayal. But the day came when, after a friend spoke to me, I confronted him with the question, "Have you and so and so been seeing each other?" Ashamed, he admitted they had, though he confessed their brief affair had ended two months earlier. He wept and begged for my forgiveness, sincerely sorry for the indiscretion. At first I was out of control with anger and shock. In outrage, I screamed and cried continuously, beating upon his chest like some mad woman. Then for five days I took to a chair, rising only to go to the bathroom or bed. I did not eat; I forgot I had children to care for. I did not brush my teeth nor comb my hair. It was bizarre, but that's how I coped.

Then despite my inability to function, I learned the most wonderful thing. In those five days in that chair, I learned that God alone is sufficient. For in a way I can only try to describe, for the entire duration, while I sat in the recliner, I sat cradled in the arms of God. I could feel His presence and His arms around me. It was as though the knowledge of Ralph's unfaithfulness was passing from my head through my whole body and finally one day exited my feet. In the time I sat in that chair, the forgiveness process was completed, and I arose five days later, loving Ralph still, ready to begin our marriage again, the past behind us. No doubt it was the Lord's holding and rocking me quietly that affected the healing. Without a doubt, He was sufficient for that dark time.

Still Ralph's mid-life crisis took a second turn a bit later. Around forty, he decided to leave his blue-collar hands-on job to retrain for a white-collar office job. This entailed three to four years of deprivation, as one year he made only eight thousand dollars. As he continued to cast about, searching for any new suitable employment opportunity, I was forced to work full-time, something I was loath to do, always desiring to be home with the boys in their growing-up years. Twice we nearly lost the house, being unable to meet the mortgage payments. In the end, we sold the place when several of its major systems needed redoing and we didn't have the funds for the repairs. From there we moved into a motel room, then to a rental, and finally back to the motel for two years.

It was only the Lord's sufficiency in the midnight hour that enabled us to purchase a home on the exact two-year date of the exit from our original home. The miracle of this timing was that the prevailing capital gains tax laws then required you reinvest any profits gained from a house sale into a new home by the two-year mark or you had to pay back all the gains, plus a penalty retroactive to the home's sale date. That would have absolutely finished us off financially, taking away the only deposit money we would ever have for another home. But we "passed papers" on our new home on the exact two-year date. God certainly wasn't early in this crisis, but as the saying goes, neither was He late, but right on time.

I've seen and appreciated God's sufficiency a multitude of times in the ensuing years. He has brought us safely through each new crisis to every matter's good and final resolution. Sufficient unto the day is the trouble therein, the scripture says (Matthew 6:34). And so it is also a venerable truth that where I once in my youth thought goodwill, a cheerful heart,

This Much I Know

stout resolution, and my own devices enough to carry the day, older, wiser now I realize when the storms of life hit, only the sufficiency of an all-loving, all-powerful, omnipresent God is enough to bring us successfully through.

The Tough Decision

> This much I know...Our God is different from mere man; His ways are not the same as men's.
>
> "For my thoughts are not your thoughts, neither are your ways my ways," declares the Lord. "As the heavens are higher than the earth, so are my ways higher than your ways and my thoughts than your thoughts."
>
> —Isaiah 55:8, 9 NIV

My aunt often quotes a television evangelist who teaches, "It's not the problem that's the problem; it's the way we view the problem that's the problem." I've seen the truth of that statement several times in my life, but perhaps never so clearly as when Ian and I were newlyweds facing our first big decision—whether to move halfway across country, changing both our jobs, and returning to live near our extended families. We lived then on the west coast in beautiful rugged Oregon, where we'd gotten our first jobs after college and settled into our first home together. The idea of a move back to the Midwest, where we'd both grown up, emerged as a topic of conversation increasingly in the first six months of marriage. But when I was of a mind to make the move, Ian wasn't. Almost perversely, when he saw merit in the move, I was unsure, of a differing mind; and we were both unsettled in the matter.

My strong feelings began to cause frustration, then resentment to grow between us. Irrational as it was, I couldn't get past the feelings, however they fluctuated. We prayed for guidance, but couldn't seem to get on the same page. Trying to match up my feelings, thoughts, and viewpoints was simply an impossibility, until God spoke directly to me and then to Ian. He told me we were going about this thing the wrong way, that His ways were not ours. Instead, He spoke of my submitting in simple obedience to His way. This meant submitting to Ian.

As new and difficult a thought as this was, I knew it to be the answer, so I began, instead of trying to figure the problem out myself, to simply pray for and listen to Ian as God directed him. In no time at all really, the situation then turned from chaos to order. As I prayed for Ian to have God's mind on the matter, and I God's heart, I was released from the bondage of decision making. I no longer felt it my job to make sure I was understood, listened to, validated and affirmed, but rather I felt the need to listen instead. I guess this was my first lesson in obedience and trust that God's design for marriage really works, and is certainly better than my own. As I worked solely on my heart, a peace was granted me and a freedom for Ian, who in turn received the answer after worshipping in church one Sunday.

In the end, we have learned that the decisions made in our marriage are not nearly as important to God as the process we go through in making them. Being right is not the same thing as being righteous. Our relationships to Him and to each other are the paramount thing. Humility, sweet surrender of our own wills, trust, and patience are godly character qualities the Lord is working into and out of us.

Once we achieve this Christlikeness to any great degree, we see the truth in the scripture that says His ways are higher than ours (Isaiah 55:9). For what could be better than having peace instead of strife, unity in spite of differing perspectives, guidance and not confusion, and above all unbroken oneness with both God and one another?

The Quiet Voice

This much I know . . . Our God still speaks.

"My sheep hear my voice . . ."
—John 10:27 KJV

When I was a very young girl, one afternoon I went to visit a neighborhood friend; I knocked on her door but no one answered, so I started back home. In her driveway, there suddenly appeared out of nowhere a man with a truck. He beckoned to me enticingly, saying, "Little girl, come see the bird I have here." I could see the beautiful bird in its cage, and I had a special affinity towards all nature, birds included, so I was sorely tempted to obey his command. But "something" in my inner self told me instead to run, and I did; I ran to safety. It was only years later that I came to know that inner voice was the Lord's, and in obeying it I found and find protection.

Fast-forwarding my life's story, a year after I married, I discovered after a round of doctoring and consultations, that my body, at twenty-five years of age, was hormonally imbalanced; I was in early menopause. The specialist said I had no chance of ever becoming pregnant, fulfilling my deep desire to be a mother. My husband and I, after adjusting to the sad news, decided to adopt two children. Two precious girls eventually became ours. When the girls were approximately two and four years old, I was at a place of contentment and stopped praying about more children.

Yet one day a strange thing happened while I was reading my Bible. Verses in Isaiah 61 came alive to me; they literally jumped off the page as I read them, and I knew the Lord was speaking to me through them. They spoke of rebuilding the ancient ruins, the desolation of many generations. I just knew instinctively they referred to the healing of my body and of the restoration of its life-giving ability. But at first I didn't tell anyone, even my husband, believing they would think me crazy. Still, because I believed them true, I did make a doctor appointment. The morning of the visit, my four-year old came to me with her Bible open and asked me read her the story that was written on those pages. It was the story of Hannah, and I knew God was confirming His prior word to me and also revealing the child would be a boy.

However, the doctor, after his examination, believed only that my hormone levels were fluctuating and needed adjustment. At my insistence—probably to humor me—he did do a pregnancy test and was flabbergasted at the results, going so far as to question the nurse as to whether it was my specimen he was looking at. He then told me to go off the hormone replacement therapy I'd been on, and I answered, "I already did—two weeks ago," as I'd felt led to stop taking the medicine. Amazed as he was though, he did caution me I'd never carry the baby to full term and shouldn't get my hopes up. Nonetheless, I trusted God and knew the doctor was wrong. Seven months later I delivered our son, who, at four pounds, was entirely healthy, although a preemie to be sure. The nurses unwittingly, with their comments, gave me a few moments of fear, but once again I opened the Bible randomly, and my eyes fell on this verse in Isaiah 65: "No longer will there be an infant who lives for just a few days." God's Word was very specific, and with it He reassured me all was well.

Up to this point in my life, God's speaking had been primarily for personal enlightenment or my encouragement, but I was being brought to the place where He would have me speak to others for their sakes as well. This required a different level of trust, for if I were wrong in imparting the word to another it could bring pain to them, shame to me, and discredit to the Lord. Then, too, prior to this point, I had only shared after the fact, but now was being brought to prophesy, or forth tell future things for God's purposes.

One night I was awakened with a 3 AM phone call—a crisis prayer need. A one-year old in the church family had been rushed to the hospital, and it was determined he needed a heart transplant to live. Again I sought the Lord. With my Bible open, in quiet prayer, confident I was in His presence and audience, I read Psalm 102. The words said, "The child will live and it be spoken of to His glory in generations to come . . . to set free those doomed to death . . . the children of thy servants will continue." It's a very serious thing to say, "Thus saith the Lord," and when I later entered the hospital room and saw the baby squirming and shaking, tubes running in and out of his body everywhere, my eyes did not tell me the baby would live. For a few days I felt a dark heaviness, as if the heavens themselves were battling for this child.

To confuse the situation further, a young woman with whom I went to the hospital, and with whom I shared the Lord's Word, had lost her own newborn baby years earlier and advised me not to do anything to give the anguished mom false hope. The baby's mother herself had asked me what to do with his clothes and crib, saying "How can I go on, expecting his sure death?" Everything pointed to that certainty. Still I finally obeyed the Lord. Stepping out in sheer faith alone, faith that I had heard Him correctly, I shared the words He'd given me. As the days continued to unfold, we saw the miraculous happen . . . a new heart given, put into place, and no sign of rejection following the implant. Today he is a healthy five-year old.

As I contemplate God's speaking to His children, I have come to understand several things. It is not a strange phenomena reserved for a few special folks, or solely reserved for Old or New Testament saints. God desires an intimate relationship with each of us today—that's a large part of why He created us, for fellowship with Himself—yet learning to hear His voice is not always easy. Generally His voice is not audible, but instead an inner confidence born of time spent alone talking to and listening for Him. He may speak in countless ways—through persons, the written word, music, nature, circumstances. He is not limited, and the ways and means of His communication are endless and varied. Another important component in understanding His voice is that we must believe with faith that He will speak before He does. Jesus Himself said with great sorrow that He could do no miracle in a certain city because of their unbelief. Then, too, we're quick to bail ourselves out of our problems with our own plans and schemes, rather than to take the time needed to seek the Lord and get His perspective. There is no quick way, no easy formula to hear from God. He alone chooses the time He'll speak and often seems in no hurry to do so.

Recently I counseled a young believer, who had an eating disorder, to seek His Word herself on the problem. She returned to me a while later excited to share He had most certainly spoken to her through a verse in Ecclesiastes, "Eat your food with gladness" (Acts 2:46). With this word, her heart was comforted and a dire situation averted. Now she is learning to go directly to Him, not necessarily to others, when she has a problem that needs addressing. Many find it amazing that the Lord God, so busy running the whole world, should deign to stoop to hear our feeble, often self-serving prayers and respond. Yet has He not said He is the same yesterday, today, and tomorrow? Surely that includes His good pleasure today to reveal Himself, His mind, and His heart to His listening child, as in days of old. And whether it's over a critical matter affecting the whole world or just a simple personal question or concern, we, believers in the one true God and His son Jesus Christ, are grateful our God isn't dumb like false gods but strives and does communicate with us by speaking in ways and words we can comprehend.

Peril on a Summer's Night

This much I know . . . Our God is always with us.

> The LORD is my strength and shield; my heart trusted in him, and I am helped: therefore my heart greatly rejoiceth; and with my song I shall praise him.
> —Psalm 28:7 KJV

One summer, my husband Ernie and I vacationed for a while in Alaska with my sister and brother-in-law, who had relocated to the "wilds," homesteading on a site with no electricity and none of the amenities normal living offers. One day, leaving from their place in Juneau, we began a trip that required riding a ferry. On the return leg of the journey, we really cut it close in terms of time. It was a Sunday evening around dusk when we pulled into the port of Wrangle—about an hour and a half ride by boat to their home. We needed to get off the ferry and quickly load groceries and lumber supplies onto the skiff—a sixteen-foot rowboat-like conveyance with a motor so we could get back by light of day, since there is no light available for traveling on the ocean waterways at night.

Before boarding the skiff, we also had to purchase some other provisions in town, including materials for a hot tub project my brother-in-law Nick was completing. Both errands were additional time stealers. It was raining, too, but that was not unusual, because the area we were in was rain forest. As we arrived in Wrangle, the day ominously began to darken with fog rolling in. Nick, a coast guardsman himself, had confidence in his ability on the water and was determined we not stay ashore for the night, but instead that we proceed homeward. We packed the boat so tightly there were only eight inches of "throw run," in which to move and two inches of water clearance from the ocean itself so heavily weighed down were we.

To make matters worse, the boat had no light on it and the sky was cloudy, appearing moonless. All the waterways up there were surrounded by small islands, each looking just like the other—and there was a twenty-foot tidal change in that particular area. Going into those waters was really dangerous. Still, early on, I wasn't afraid, because Nick, standing at the back of the boat, seemed so confident, so sure we'd soon come to the buoy marker he knew to be around there. All our eyes were peeled, but we didn't sight it until it was almost eight feet away, because of the fog closing in. Under normal conditions we'd have spied it way off in the distance. Not long after that, we came to a patch of seaweed. He cut the engine low, but it seized up anyway, wrapping around the "intake," and it died.

Sensing danger, I suggested to Nick we just row to the side and sleep overnight, but he would have none of that, as he didn't have his gun with him and knew this to be bear country. It was still twenty miles to their property at this point, and we were totally in the middle of nowhere and at the mercy of anything and everything. With the engine out and having no other choice, the men began rowing the boat, and the dogs we had aboard began to howl. I had never before been in a situation remotely similar—so dire—and had no idea what to do. I didn't even know how to pray. With no other boats around I knew no help from man was available. So, as the guys rowed, my sister and I prayed simply that the Lord would help us, and we began singing hymns. After a while Nick suggested we try the engine again and "miraculously" it started up, so we putsed the remaining distance, going slowly along with no wake. We couldn't go at a good clip, because it was totally dark and we'd hit rocks, which were virtually everywhere around us. When we arrived at their cove, unable to see a thing for the pitch blackness of night, because they didn't have a dock, we put the motor up and pushed the boat in blindly. Looking back now, I see that the Lord's presence gave us a sense of peace, in spite of the awful realities of the situation. Despite the danger, we never panicked—nor were we overwhelmed with paralyzing fear. This fact alone is amazing, as an unlighted, over-packed, small boat on an unpredictable ocean with big swells on a foggy night is a recipe for disaster. Truly anything could have happened to us, and no one would have even known. I often think back to this experience and remember what I learned from it . . . that our God is always present in times of crisis, if we will but pray and praise, He will carry us safely through life's uncertain waters to the safety of the shore.

Fountain in Hawaii

> This much I know . . . Our God is a well of living water.
>
> But whosoever drinks from the water I give him shall never thirst again but the water I shall give him will become in him a well springing up to everlasting life.
>
> —John 4:14 KJV

For about ten years I was a baby Christian, living off pabulum, just content to know a Bible truth in my head. Then came a time when I began to desire meat and to live out the knowledge I'd gained, to have it be more than mere words. It was as if a veil were lifted from my eyes. I saw the futility of having answers to life's problems but not being able to implement them. I began to sense God wanting now to get inside of me and produce change there, rather than work just on the external, my outward behavior. I hadn't had a lot of trouble with the externals, but this inside work was new ground and tougher, for I had many inner struggles and conflicts. It was as if God were saying, "I have plans for you, but you have to go deeper with Me."

This began a several-year process of learning to spend time with Him alone in the secret place—often sitting quietly for periods of time, simply awaiting His voice. Because I'd been so parched, so dry, prior to this, though in truth I hadn't realized it, I really desired this new spiritual exercise. Still I found it hard to discipline myself to do it. By nature I'm a Martha—a doer, a fixer, quick to act. To learn to find my center as Mary did, not in what she did but in what she was, taking her place regularly at the Master's feet, was hard. I wanted to produce, not perceive, and while both have their place, Jesus did say of Mary, "She has chosen the good part."

Sitting at all, let alone quietly, learning of and to enjoy Him, making Him alone my focus was far from a natural process. Actually I found it uncomfortable, because I had to "cease from my labors" and come face-to-face with my true self. I was forced to look at all the warts and blemishes on my soul and, more to the point, deal with them. Even beginning the process was much like a newborn baby learning to suckle. I could hardly latch on, never mind feed. But learn I did to give Him my whole undivided attention and to not reject silence, His or mine, nor correction if He spoke of needed change. All the rooms of my heart I'd heretofore barred Him from were opened, and He was doing a big cleaning job on them. Unfortunately, this process cannot be rushed and was painful at times as I saw my true state before Him. But always graciously, lovingly, He led me on.

I read a lot during this period—mostly stories and books about the great men and women of faith and of the historic church, only to find that they too had been in the same school house, learning to draw from His cistern rather than from their own wells, learning further His thoughts and heart and voice. From here I gained an expanded vision, understanding, and love for the work He was doing in the world, not just my small corner of it. As the bigger picture emerged and became my desire, I was led into more intimate worship and deeper prayer. Intersession now began in earnest. No longer were my prayers primarily for myself and our family needs, though those were certainly legitimate requests. I was not so much seeking His hand as His face and was almost in travail as love for mankind was birthed in me. I guess I could say He gave me a purer, more Christlike, love for His sake, and I desired to live out my life in holiness for His purposes.

I was immersed in the sanctification (setting apart) process, which I understand to be a deeper understanding and outworking of His character and will, through my surrender and cooperation with the Holy Spirit. It's a death to the soul part of us—to our fleshly appetites. It's what John the Baptist spoke of when he said, "I must decrease; He must increase" (John 3:30 KJV). One result of this is a growing awareness at all times of His presence, and then also a new sensing of His prompting. We recognize more quickly when we're grieving Him, when we sin, and now biblical sorrow over our sin, for we see how it hurts Him and not just how it affects us. Because we have an expanded awareness of His grace, mercy, and love, we no longer take our sin casually. Also there's a new deeper appreciation for the cross. To say it another way, the process was like drinking deep living waters.

While in Hawaii recently for our twenty-fifth anniversary, I chanced one day to sit by a fountain and watch its endless flow of fresh water. Lulled by the continuous soft sound of falling water, I understood my new relationship with the Lord to be like this. First I had to take time apart to sit and be still to appreciate the fountain site. Then as it played quietly on my senses, I entered into its endless capacity to refresh, from its deep hidden source. In a real sense, I chose the degree to which I entered into its delights. It was there for all to enjoy 24/7, but only by my conscious choice and discipline was I blessed by it. Practically speaking, the longer

I allowed the waters to do their work, the better equipped I was after leaving its presence to face the problems in my life with peace.

For like many others at our stage of life, we faced some biggies, as our three children were crossing from childhood into adulthood. Our old tendencies in crisis situations were to vocalize our displeasure and to bring pressure upon the erring child to shape up. Now instead I had a new confidence that God, alone, was in control. Despite the outward circumstances of any situation, we found that like Mary, sitting at the Lord's feet quietly, praising the One who had the solutions to our troubles, we received wisdom not our own, in addition to a calm with which to ride out the storm. In fasting and prayer, we often even found serenity. Instead of frantically begging and commanding God to intervene in the way we thought best, we could instead pray deep Spirit-led intercessory prayers with a quiet confidence, awaiting His presence to be manifest. I was learning to differentiate between regular prayer and true intercessory prayer.

It seems to me that intersession is a gut-wrenching form of prayer on another's behalf that bypasses the mind, as if it were coming from another place through the will and power of the Holy Spirit Himself, rather than one's own more simple thoughts. Many times in intersession, you pray hard things you'd not before dared, and often the prayer is based on a scripture. It can be a time of travail, prevailing prayer. Prior to this deeper entering in, where we're drinking from living waters, I was often despairing, my spiritual strength sapped, fervently focused primarily on myself. I had no confidence in His ability and willingness to undertake in the difficulty. Now in the secret place I was learning to release concerns to Him and drink refreshing waters of forgiveness and hope.

No longer did I endlessly recount my shortcomings—though they were many—but instead saw His wonder-working power to bring good resolution to the issues. If I'd occasionally revert back to the old ways, to self solutions, it was like drinking brackish, warm waters from stagnant pools. My thirst there was never really slaked, so I was drawn of necessity back to His deeper well continually. I had come increasingly into a better alignment with God's heart and mind. I found primarily on His heart was my learning to rest in Him, for there is a rest for the people of God this side of heaven and in the midst of our toil. The Sabbath is the one day God invites us to cease from work and to worship and be restored, and it is mainly for our sakes, not His, that He gave us this command. If we fail to heed it, we begin the new week unrefreshed, unfit to meet its demands. So we must always be pursuing Him, even as He is always pursuing us.

In 2 Chronicles 15:2, the prophet Asa reminds us, "The LORD is with you while ye be with him." In other words, you will find Him when you seek Him with all your heart (Jeremiah 29:13). This, of course, is a bit of a paradox, as the Lord promises to be with us always, to never leave us. A proper understanding of the meshing of these two truths is perhaps that one promise is positional, doctrinally true, and the other is our practical every day state, in which we work the truth through to its intended outcome.

Most recently we've experienced the joy of drinking from His living waters in conjunction with our elder son's decision to join the US Marines. He had arrived at a point prior to enlisting to see his life was going nowhere. Endless partying and a succession of dead-end jobs weren't bringing fulfillment. Having interceded for him frequently, and abiding in the Lord, we felt peace when he told us he'd been recruited. Strange this peace, except for the Lord, because certainly these are troubled days for all military personnel, their family and loved ones, Iraq being such a volatile place and very probably the country of his deployment. But having truly beforehand released him and his life to the Lord, as opposed to having only dedicated him to the Lord while a child, we are now positioned to watch expectantly as the Lord fulfills His purposes in Jeremy's life. And almost like a gift, three days after a time of fasting for him, Jeremy called to reassure us he was back on the narrow way, having turned from the prodigal path.

Now my challenge is to continue to drink from the deeper living waters. The invitation is always extended, the choice mine. I know the difference now, and more's the pity if I forsake the life-giving refreshment His well provides for the warm unsatisfying waters I can provide myself.

A Dynamic Finish

This much I know . . . Our God provides "everything plus" to fulfill His purposes.

> Now to him who is able to do immeasurably more than all we ask or imagine, according to his power that is at work in us, to him be glory in the church and in Christ Jesus throughout all generations, for ever and ever! Amen.
> —Ephesians 3:20, 21 NIV

Though we have known God as Jehovah-Jirah—my provider—for many years, recently we've had a dramatic demonstration of His miracle-working power and timely provision. Both my husband and I, in the golden years of life, made the decision in retirement not to simply fill the remaining years with personal enjoyments, but instead to continue to remain open to whatever the will of God is for us, wanting our latter years to be as fruitful as our earlier ones.

Our story really began twelve years ago, when we first started taking winter vacations in Cancun. The warmth and beauty of Mexico so enchanted us that we bought a one-week timeshare and returned yearly to enjoy its offerings. In 2001, before the annual visit, we began praying that this year's vacation be more than just a week of refreshment—that God would use us in some way that served and pleased Himself. We had no idea what that prayer would yield, how far-reaching its effects would be.

On one of the first days there, while sunning on the beach we "chanced," in God's providential design, to meet a fellah who offered to take us snorkeling in his boat. I asked if we could do that tomorrow instead, but his reply was, "No, tomorrow I go to the orphanage." Intrigued, I inquired if we could go with Him. He agreed, so the following day we viewed that facility and grounds and met its precious houseparents/CEOs and the fifty-two resident children.

Back home in Connecticut the Sunday morning of our return, but before church, a woman called us about some matter, and in the course of the conversation asked why we had not invited her to accompany us to Mexico, as she spoke the language and was of Spanish descent. A short while later that same morning, a second person came to us, expressing interest in going with us when we returned. Surprised but encouraged by these happenings, we threw out an open invitation for an informal meeting in our home to see whether there were others also who had interest in the orphanage project. Twenty-seven people attended that first meeting, and we began to sense God at work. We checked with Jovita and Edwardo, the orphanage heads, to find out their specific needs and began planning a return mission trip for the next summer.

As time drew near for our actual departure date, my husband decided to call the airline about a possible flight change. We had previously booked tickets for ten people departing Newark, New Jersey, on July 3. Because Newark is several hours from our homes, and traffic on a summer holiday weekend extra challenging, he asked if it were at all possible to make a change . . . to fly out of Bradley International Airport in Windsor Locks, Connecticut, instead. The airport representative in return replied simply, "Oh yes, we can make that change. We have ten seats available on a flight from Hartford (just forty-five minutes from us) at no extra cost." That was a huge blessing, as it meant no additional financial burden for anyone. And so began God's exceeding abundances. The morning of our trip, when Sam left for his early morning walk, only five folks had committed to the trip but by the time he came back home, we had the full complement of ten—exactly the number he had been led to reserve for.

Seated on the plane, one of our members, a sixteen-year-old boy, came to us overjoyed to share his story. It seems he had asked God to confirm to him that this trip was for him, was indeed of God, by allowing one of our group to ride first class. Shortly after boarding, out of the blue, a woman in our party was called up front by the stewardess and reseated in first class. We had also prayed that somehow the thirty pieces of luggage we traveled with would go through customs unopened, so to avoid needless hassle and additional tariffs. Amazingly, all thirty pieces passed through unopened.

Yet another "exceeding abundantly" (Ephesians 3:20) materialized just prior to the actual trip, when Sam called our timeshare representative at headquarters to inquire about possible housing for us all. The woman who answered the phone "just happened" to be the actual head of the organization, and when he told her we needed two two-bedroom condos, she had and offered them free of charge! Her only comment was, "Isn't God good." We were seeing repeatedly God's generous provision for the work He had ordained, how He Himself undergirded ministry, bringing exactly what was needed to it in the perfect time.

Another wondrous occurrence happened about a week before that trip. I was awakened in the night by the Lord and had the strange thought to "buy the children underwear." The thought kept coming to me, so in simple obedience, the next day I went to Wal-Mart and purchased fifty-two sets of underwear. Once down in Mexico, I said to Jovita, "This is the strangest thing, but I brought new underwear for all the kids." She immediately burst into tears—sharing that the children were constantly given second-hand clothing, but she herself had just been praying for new underwear for each. God's exceeding kindness still thrills me, as I recall how He worked in even this small detail.

Since that time two years ago, we've been continuously involved in the orphanage work, watching the Lord bring to it those who can specifically help meet its ongoing needs—particularly in the areas of teaching English, music, computer, and Bible. One final precious blessing we're seeing is that of the generations picking up the baton. Our daughter and grandchildren have taken an interest and plan to accompany us on future trips. Though I know things don't always come together in such a dramatic way, when I recall all the "exceeding abundancies" God did as we started this particular work, I can only believe it is to His glory. What a privilege we'd have missed if we'd simply retired, living solely to pleasure ourselves, not remaining open to His will and work for us.

Without a Song

This much I know . . . Our God is worth it.

My ears had heard of you but now my eyes have seen you.

—Job 42:5 NIV

Three years ago, I was told by my surgeon there was a fifty-fifty chance that I would never sing again. Music brings me joy, lifts my spirit, and drives me to the throne of God, so I could not understand why God would choose to take something from me that I was using for him. I love to sing, and I love to sing praises to Him. As limited human beings, though, we do not have the ability to judge the creator of heaven and earth or even ask Him why, but this much I know . . . for sure I didn't like it.

The news of my cancer came at a difficult time in my life. I was newly married and had two small children to care for. Shortly after discovering the cancer through a biopsy, I was told to embark on a series of radiation treatments and crazy diets. That was scary enough, but the thought of losing my voice was the real kicker. As I sat in my living room one afternoon trying to make sense of everything, I finally realized that I just couldn't put the pieces together. From my perspective, they didn't fit, and I came to accept the fact that I couldn't see the big picture because God didn't want me to. He just wanted me to trust. In Isaiah 55:8-9, it says, "'For my thoughts are not your thoughts, neither are your ways my ways,' declares the Lord. 'Just as the heavens are higher than the earth, so are my ways higher than your ways and my thoughts than your thoughts.'"

God wasn't going to fit into the box that I wanted Him to and had foolishly created for Him. He is much too big and His knowledge is much too vast for my finite mind to comprehend. All I could do was to place everything into His hands: my hurt, my questions, my life. This realization was painstaking. It came through many tears, as I recognized and yielded to the truth that I could not fix my problems as I had done so many times before. I had only two choices—I could live a bitter life or I could trust that God knew what He was doing. I chose the latter, and though surrender is hardly ever easy, God is faithful, and what He gives in return for our giving up control is incomparable.

He gave me a beautiful gift that day. As I humbled myself and submitted to His ways, He pulled me closer and I began to experience him more fully. In the epilogue of the book of Job, Job cries, "Now my eyes have seen you." This declaration came after he had lost his children, his livelihood, his riches, and his health, and more importantly, before he knew God was going to restore them all back. I realized that if I could experience the presence of God in such a personal and intimate way by bowing before Him and saying, "Your will be done," that I would have gained much—even if I never sang a note again for the rest of my life. That day, as I cried out to God, He wrapped His arms around me so tightly I swore I physically felt the touch. Never before and never since have I felt that close to the Lord. It was my pain that brought me there, but it was His hand that lifted me up to an extraordinary place of fellowship, and He gave me a glimpse of His precious face. And that made it all worth it.

Several years have passed since those difficult days, and I did not lose my voice. Instead today I have the privilege sometimes of even singing to and for Him in public offerings. I count that pure joy, but more important still is the remembrance of personally experiencing Him and His touch in my darkest hour.

But He Could Leave

> This much I know . . . Our God is omnipresent, or said another way . . . always there.
>
> Where can I go from your Spirit? . . . If I go up to the heavens, you are there; if I make my bed in the depths, you are there. If I rise on the wings of the dawn, if I settle on the far side of the sea, even there your hand will guide me, your right hand will hold me fast.
> —Psalm 139:7-10 NIV

Growing up, I was aware of there being a God and of His seeing me, but I thought He was far away, holy, unapproachable, and mean. Perhaps my understanding was limited because we attended a French church where no English was spoken, so I really had no formal training on religious things. I do remember at fourteen wondering what sin was—I had heard the word used. One time I stole a deck of cards from Woolworth's, the local five and dime store, and a religious man told me not to worry—that my stealing wasn't a sin because Woolworth's was a chain store. I guess the implication was they could easily cover the loss; but even as a young child, that didn't sound quite right. Still I knew little of God's law then and for many years to come. It wasn't until I was married several years, had children, and worked in our own tool business by my husband's side that I came to understand that God is knowable, always present, loving, and kind.

At a certain point in time I needed Him desperately, because after several years of marriage, my husband announced out of the blue one night that he "wanted out." Apparently he'd been flirting with temptation for a while and also was involved with alcohol. Yet I loved him dearly and could not imagine him leaving us. Unable to sleep many nights, I began to cry out to God these simple words, "Where are you?" After about two weeks of such carryings on, around 3 AM, I suddenly remembered a book I'd sent for a while back. Actually I'd ordered it for my husband, and when it was delivered, I'd just shoved it unopened into a drawer somewhere. Now I went to find it, tore the package wrapping off and began to read for the first time the words of life. But even then I didn't realize that God had been there all along and had allowed this book to be there for me in my hour of desperation. That understanding would come later.

The book contained life stories, testimonies, of real life people who had real life problems just like mine—and had found God to be the answer to those problems. They found Him not only to have the answers, but to Himself be their answer. As I read the words on the pages of the little book, they came alive. I continued to cry out, to read and search in the only way I knew, with all my heart. My search was simple, desperate, and definitely sincere.

I read in the book about Revelation 3:20, which says He stands at the door and knocks—as if to ask permission to enter. I was still so ignorant spiritually that I thought that meant a literal door, not the entrance to my heart. So at 4 AM that night, I went to the front door of our house, opened it wide, and asked Him to come in. When I did that, at that exact moment, His presence overwhelmed me and I started to shake and cry out, "Oh God." He spoke back, and somehow I knew it was His voice saying, "You're going to be alright." A degree of peace enveloped me so that I no longer even cared if my husband left or not. I felt so safe, and the feeling continued for weeks. From that day to this (and my husband never did leave us, but instead in time became a godly Christian and strong family man), the Lord has restored our love. I've learned to spend time alone with the Lord each day, and in doing so, have sensed His nearness and continuing presence in every circumstance of life since that night. It really amazes me that a God who is holy, mighty and powerful, in charge of running the whole world, is so approachable and ready to love us without reserve and measure. Most of all I wonder that we can have His abiding presence just by asking for it. It's a shame my ignorance and formal religion kept me from that joy for so many years, but it's also nothing short of wonderful that I found him in my hour of desperation by simply earnestly seeking Him in the only simple way I knew.

Absolutely Lost

This much I know . . . Our God alone has the answers to life's problems.

My son, attend to my words; incline thy ears unto my sayings . . . For they are life unto those who find them, and health to all their flesh.
—Proverbs 4:20, 22 KJV

At age fourteen, my quiet somewhat normal life began spinning out off control when I was hospitalized with an unknown digestive problem. The doctors were unable to discover its source, finally settling on a colitis-like disease, which brings with it no real hope for cure, only possible remission. Symptoms persisted; I felt sick most of the time and suffered the loss of the general well-being I'd always before enjoyed. Somehow I got through my high school years, but when divorce hit my family, the emotional toll of ongoing problems became overwhelming. I sought answers from eight doctors and as many medicines and solace from others, who unfortunately, though kind and caring, had no answers for my problems either. At a precipice at age twenty, life became unbearable and a strange confluence of events left me nowhere to live but the home of relatives half a continent away. Truth be told, of all the folks I'd have chosen to live with, they'd have been the very last. My family and I had often laughed behind their backs at their simplistic Christianity and silly old-fashioned biblical ways. We had also seen them as "holier than thou" folks, who steadfastly maintained only God had answers to life's sticky problems, and they were willing to share them. Oh, how willing they were to share them—nauseatingly willing. Perhaps we hated that most of all.

But sick as I was, desperately needing change, and in no position to effect it myself, I relocated one thousand eight hundred miles east of my birthplace and took up residence with my aunt and uncle. Shortly after my arrival, I began attending a Bible-believing church for the first time in my life. Immediately, I was accepted as one of the church family. Disarmed by their unconditional love and acceptance, my walls began to crumble. I began to learn how to apply God's written Word in the Bible to the everyday situations in my life. Little by little, my anxiety and panic attacks subsided, and one by one over the next year, I set aside my medicines. As my mind healed, to a large degree my body also healed.

My focus turned outward, and I began serve the Lord and others, instead of just myself. Strangely my own needs were met as I paid less attention to them—one of God's little secrets—a new way to live, and bit by bit, it freed me from the bondage by which I'd formerly been held. As I renewed my mind in Christ's Word, I had a freedom from having to care for myself. The Lord Himself cared for me. Specifically He provided me a decent local job, use of a car, free room and board, healthy caring peers and mentors, and eventually a college acceptance to study nursing. In short order followed a special guy, an engagement ring, wedding plans, a college degree, and a high paying job—all the good things

I'd previously wanted, but had been unable to obtain on my own.

There's a little story—made into a video series—in which Bruce Wilkerson shares about three chairs, depicting the various places we as Christians occupy. I can identify with his analogy, because prior to coming east I'd sat in the second chair. I was a believer, but seeking "my own stuff"— what I believed I deserved and wanted, in a way and timeframe that pleased me. My focus was primarily myself, my goals, and most especially my feelings. Now I struggle to sit in the first chair—that of the committed Christian, who in simple childlike trust obeys the Lord, letting Him care for his needs and choosing his portion. I desire to remain preoccupied with Him and His kingdom, seeking those things above all else. My feelings, once the engine on the train, are now rightly the caboose. There is a great peace I enjoy in this simple obedience and the faith it brings. It's a marvelous, supernatural way to live and excels all others. I can most assuredly say God has the answers to my and your problems. If in life you've reached a place where it's not working, I encourage you to give it all to Him—He'll take it and make something wonderful of it when you do.

To the Journey's End

> This much I know . . . Our God will carry us in times of difficulty.
>
> Even unto old age I am He who will carry you.
> —Isaiah 46:4 KJV

From my earliest recollection, my mother had painful, crippling rheumatoid arthritis. It was so bad that her hair turned snow white by age thirty-five. When I was just five, my grandmother died and my mother had to return to Canada for the funeral. She took both my newborn sister and me with her alone on the train from northwest Connecticut to New Brunswick. This was the first time I ever saw the Lord "carry" anyone. Even at that tender age, I marveled at how she, in such pain, could take that long trip and manage with such grace. Somehow I recognized the significance of it, though I was really too young to comprehend its full truth and implications for my own life. This was a time of great sadness and difficulty, yet my mother never once complained—instead believing and behaving in a way that acknowledged God is in control and that He is always with us.

Less than two years later, my older brother was killed. Once again I watched mom go through a terrible time with amazing grace. There was no despair in her voice, sadness yes, as if she were physically exhausted—as if she were touching the pain but not lost in it. Increasingly, she spent more time in bed, because the arthritis was debilitating. She once explained to us that before she'd become a Christian, she'd had a terrible temper and anger problem, but God had dealt with that in her life to the point that when we knew her we could hardly believe she'd ever had that problem. She was calm and sweet-spirited, never lashing out at anyone or any situation, including her bedridden condition and constant limitations. She actually told me once that had she not had the arthritis affliction, she would not have developed in her relationship with the Lord and so been able to go through the years gracefully. She quoted a favorite Bible verse in Psalm 119 about affliction being given us by God, in love, for our benefit. Therefore, she spent many an hour pressed into Him alone in study and prayer, and came out from that quiet place strong in her faith and full of sweetness.

I didn't actually experience God's carrying me until I married and faced devastating unexpected news one day. I'd been married only six years when my husband was diagnosed with Hodgkin's lymphoma. It was suddenly my time to experience God's ability to take me through deep waters. John's illness and diagnosis came quickly—like a body slam—within the space of one month. One day he seemed well, the next he was hospitalized, facing a battery of tests with dire results. My mind at the very first raced with thoughts of becoming a widow and single mom in my young twenties. Our first child was just a few months old. When our thoughts are so negative, they can really pull us down under, but God didn't allow that to happen to me. When I would get into bed at night and find it difficult to fall asleep, my thoughts crowding in quickly and replaying like a stuck record, He would cradle me; and I would fall asleep, and amazingly, awaken refreshed with a strong sense He was in control. I felt this so much that I would be able to do each day all that needed to be done. It was as if I was in a mode where I could see myself outside of myself and so behave without being overwrought, no doubt the many faith-filled prayers of others contributed to my sense of being carried. I know God always has us in His hand, but it's in the deep waters I sensed His presence in the most real way.

Continuing along that road, through the years God has used ill health a great deal in our family as a tool to conform us to the image of His son. A recent example is that of our elder daughter's battle with Lyme disease. Had anyone told me five years ago that we'd not only watch her nearly slip away before our very eyes, but also face huge expenses — $250 a day for IV treatments for four years, without insurance, as we live solely by faith, having been denied affordable coverage because of John's prior cancer, I'd have said the situation was very simply impossible. Yet, God has met our every need as it evolved, miraculously, faithfully, and on time. On paper, looking at the finances, anyone would have said, "You're sunk," but we did not sink; God "carried us" over. Because John is in full-time Christian service, we live differently from many. We live "by faith"—instead of from paycheck to paycheck, we live by whatever the Lord sends our way, monies mostly passing first through the hands of friends and other believers who give to God's work. It's amazing but true that after twenty-five years of marriage, living solely dependent upon the Lord's provision, we now own our own home outright, have seen our children educated and all their needs met, have never lacked proper vehicles, and have enjoyed many extras, like travel and vacations.

Our house is a perfect example of the Lord's supernatural provision. Early in our marriage, having two children and being heavily involved in hospitality, we decided to look for a home. We house-hunted and found a suitable place, only to be told by the bank we did not qualify for a mortgage loan because we did not have a guaranteed income. We went back to the Lord, prayed simply asking for His will, as we were willing to continue to rent if He desired it, but had such a strong desire to own that we felt homeownership was of Him. Still we gave Him the choice and about that time a businessman walked up to John one day at a meeting, and out of nowhere, said the following, "If you ever need a loan, I'd be happy to give you one at a low interest." God did use this man to finance our home. Here again, though we've learned not to get our eyes on a person as our source, but the Lord himself, and to let Him take us wherever He desires, give us whatever He chooses, and of course in it all to recognize the difference between wants and needs.

I remember clearly the day John met the postman in his delivery, and the man commented, "You must work nights. You're always out collecting the mail when I come."

"No, I work for the Lord," John told him, to which the man looked at him like he was twelve cookies short of a dozen. So in a step of faith at that moment, John said to the postman "We live by faith. For example, you have just come with a delivery today. Give me my mail." And in that day's mail there "just happened to be" two checks. Many days there aren't any. But John proceeded to open one and told him "You see I don't even know this person, but somehow he's heard of our work and sent a gift." The postman drove away amazed. But we aren't amazed, only thankful and trusting for His continual care, that carries us from provision to provision and back again.

One other big area we've been "carried" in is the area of sustained loss of loved ones. In a two-year period around the turn of the millennium, we lost three aging parents, one aunt, and a sister, all of whom had lived in our area and to and for whom we had some degree of responsibility. This was the same time frame in which our daughter contracted Lyme disease, so we were not just dealing with that difficulty but also facing the end of life's journeys with our parents and sister and aunt. Yet in the midst of burying one loved one after another, we had abiding hope and assurance of being reunited in heaven one day, so even our sorrowing was limited by that truth. Also, God did finally allow us confirmation of our daughters' disease, information for which we vigilantly sought and long awaited. The confirmation actually was a great encouragement, as prior to that she was so ill many days, with no hope for treatment because they couldn't figure out what she had—that she simply lay on the couch, not having the strength to arise, and sank into a profound depression. But with the diagnosis and following treatments, she is stronger now, even engaged to be married this summer. She recognizes her illness as one of God's tools for equipping her for a life of service for Him, and in spite of the illness preventing her from attending college for an academic course of study, she says she's actually been in God's spiritual university training for eternity, and that training is of inestimable value.

In truth our history with God over the past twenty-five years has been one of being carried, then carried, then carried again. He has promised to be there even until and through the graying years, which are beginning now for us. At my mother's bedside, after a lengthy coma, and just days before her passing from life to life, she awoke to tell us she'd "just seen and talked with an angel." Another friend's husband heard Jesus Himself speak to him just before dying. These reports, plus the aggregate of met needs down through the years, assure us God most certainly will continue to carry us all the way through this life and safely into the next.

All That Is Mine

This much I know . . . Our God is a giving God, a generous God.

> Praise the LORD, O my soul, and forget not all his benefits.
> —Psalm 103:2 NIV

Several years ago my husband gave back the vice presidency position in the company where he worked, so he could be employed in a lesser capacity, believing less to be more in our lives, and to work, as The Peter Principle espouses, at the level most comfortable for and suited to him as an individual. Time progressed, and years later, he did take a "promotion," which included a raise in salary. What we didn't know then, no one bothered to tell us, was that it also entitled him to another week's vacation, plus several perks, including free mailing privileges and a company credit card. So for a few years, our ignorance meant those benefits were lost to us. The same thing happened to us spiritually.

For many years as young believers, we knew only that being born again gave us a guaranteed place in heaven one day, and our sins were forgiven. It was with great joy, and some surprise, we discovered one day that there was a whole "benefits package" available to us as God's kids. Included therein were hundreds of promises, some in the health area, some for daily provision, some for added strength, comfort, guidance, favor with man, and best of all, His continuing presence and nearness. We learned in addition He offered our lives direction, peace, significance, and supernatural incite. It took some time for us to read the manual and discover all our benefits, but as we did each became ours. As ignorance was replaced by knowledge, we came to understand what a generous employer the Lord really is. We as His servants share in all that is His.

It is not inaccurate to say our benefits are both in and "out of this world." I shudder to think how it is possible, just as with my husband's earthly employer, we could theoretically have all these options and provisions, and yet through ignorance of one kind or another not enjoy them practically. To make the generosity of God to no avail is an awful thought. I can't imagine His sadness, as well as our own, to arrive in heaven one day to be shown all He'd had for us here on earth that was laid waste . . . all His great generosity had come to naught, simply because we hadn't known of its availability.

Yet Another Opportunity

> This much I know... Our God is the God of third chances.

> He who has begun a good work in you will continue it til the day of Christ Jesus.
> —Philippians 1:6 KJV

In the church in which I grew up, the good news of Christ's death on the cross was presented primarily in a scary way. The message centered on sin and hell more so than on heaven and God's grace. Yet at fourteen, while at a Bible conference, when the truth was explained in terms of God's love—much like a suitor seeking a loving wife, I received the Lord as my personal savior. Looking back, the relevance of this approach in my life seems prophetic, as my greatest desire was then and is now to give and receive love within the relationship of marriage, a marriage similar to that modeled for me by my parents.

So at age eighteen when I met Barry, after a short courtship, and with my parents' blessing, we married. It didn't take long to discover I had not chosen wisely. After the fact Barry, showed himself to have a violent temper, to be irresponsible, unable to settle into one job, and eventually to be unfaithful. Despite my prayers and cries to the Lord, things never really got better. We moved probably ten times in eleven years, because he kept thinking the grass was greener elsewhere—that the situation, not him, was the problem. Naturally there were numerous financial problems also.

The wedge between us was a huge gulf, widening with each passing month. After a while Barry was staying away from the house, increasingly doing things of which I had no idea. What remained of our family and church life was a big façade. Finally he moved into a motel, and I discovered there was another woman in his life. Within two months of this time, he filed for a divorce that went through quickly.

There was one blessing that did result from our union; that was our son Alan. But even love for Alan couldn't save the marriage. My nine-year struggle, hiding abuse and neglect, was over when Barry left, maintaining it "wasn't my, but his" problem. We hoped and even expected he'd come to his senses, like the prodigal son, but he didn't. I was left feeling a failure, angry at myself, thinking I should have been the one to leave because of the abuse. Perhaps, I thought, if I'd have left earlier, the outcome would have been different. Then, too, I was confused and disappointed with God, because He hadn't answered my prayers and I knew He could have. He could have changed Barry's heart I reasoned. I didn't then fully understand that God has given us free will and, despite prayer to the contrary, will not overrun one's will if that one decides to seek his own rather than the Lord's will.

The next few years, though still loved and accepted by family and friends, the stigma of divorce caused me untold embarrassment. At the same time, I began to seek and find a deeper relationship in the Lord, with His becoming like a husband to me. Yet I also was really hurting then for Alan, who early on felt abandoned and was so afraid to go to bed alone that for months he slept in a sleeping bag at the foot of my bed. At the least it was a confusing and difficult time for him, not helped by the fact Barry remarried quickly and Alan was required to go on every other weekend visits with his father, new stepmother, and her three children from a previous marriage.

Then, too, I wasn't in a healthy place so as to help him. I was still so distressed, my head wasn't on straight, so to speak, and I was taking sleeping pills just to get to sleep nights. Three years passed somehow, until the day I met another man, not a Christian, and began dating him out of loneliness. Fearful I would never marry again, I had begun to look for someone with whom to share some physical contact and companionship. Fortunately, I quickly realized this fellah wasn't the right one, broke off the relationship, and shortly thereafter Fred entered my life.

He was older than I and appeared very different from Barry, in that he seemed mature, soft-spoken, sensible, strong, and reasonable, with a secure job and condo. Because of his personality type, I thought he was growing in the Lord, so after dating for one year and after premarital counseling, we made our commitments legal and married. Looking back, I see there were signs for future trouble I didn't pick up on. Though he didn't dislike Alan, he didn't warm up to him either, and his other personal relationships were poor. Actually he had no friends at all. I overlooked these two red flags, issues seemingly unimportant enough to pray about and pursue more fully. Instead of waiting for God to shine His truth upon them, for they were to become huge issues, later I simply disregarded them . . . to my future detriment. Fred's previously perfunctory behavior toward Alan before marriage afterward turned quickly to a cold hatred and abuse. He never did own responsibility for any failure in any area of his life, especially with Alan, and I could see clearly I had been "naïve" in not pursuing the red flag issues before committing to him so wholly.

His frustration with life and his temper came out on my son. The cycle started again, only this time the abuser was not my son's biological, legal father. There was lots of yelling and some hitting. Fred admitted he hated Alan and didn't want him living with us any longer. So Alan packed his bags and moved out to live with his grandparents. My motivation for not following him was the knowledge that God would take care of him (his grandparents loved him deeply and could provide him a stable environment), and I needed to be faithful to the marital vow I'd taken seriously before the Lord . . . but truly after this point things continued to decline seriously. Fred tried to separate Alan and me totally, not even telling me when Alan phoned—and to separate me from my family as well—people whom he viewed as the source of all our problems.

Yet Fred communicated less and less with me anyway, sometimes going months at a time not speaking, sleeping in a separate bedroom and working out of different levels of the house by day, so as to avoid interaction. When the counselor we saw for a while, using discernment, told him he had to go to the Lord to the foot of the cross with the problems, he stormed out, had one more session, and then refused to pay for me to continue counseling. The next three years I mainly faked it. Strangely enough, though, as our relationship continued to spiral downward, mine with the Lord soared. I didn't blame God this time. I was in a different place from before, and I truly believed God had allowed us to marry for His good purposes, but this man simply wouldn't give up control of his life to the Lord. I just continued to pray the Lord would change my heart and help me to love him unconditionally, with God's agape (giving) love. But emotionally we kept growing further and further apart, until one day amazingly he suggested a "new beginning."

This entailed a move 1800 miles away from our home and family—to Florida. Running away from troubled relationships and situations is never helpful, so it was no surprise Fred's temper, foul mouth, and anger continued to worsen and escalate once we were in Florida, to the point that I, as its sole victim, became clinically depressed. I was carrying a lot of shame, though not guilt as I had honestly done everything I knew to do before and as unto the Lord. On the verge of hospitalization after several months, I flew back north for a four-month trial separation, hoping Fred would realize my desperation and get help. Prior to this point, I had never, regardless of the pain, cruelty, or dysfunction, withdrawn myself from him. Instead, I had struggled to remain positive and active in reaching out in love, no matter his treatment or response to me. Every morning I'd begin my day by asking God for His love, with which to love this man as Christ loves the church, and somehow the Lord's grace had been sufficient for that time and need, though ultimately even that grace couldn't save the marriage.

I told Fred I wasn't going to divorce—believing that wasn't biblical—but instead intended to live separated. He then announced he had no intention of living so; he had already begun a new relationship. In short order he filed for divorce. Divorced for a second time, I decided to dedicate myself solely to the Lord, to live as a single woman until death or until Jesus returns to earth for us as promised. Actually I was content to do so, the prior turmoil ended.

Amazingly, no matter how many times we fail, the apostle Paul tells us that God never stops working out His good plans for and through us, if we are submitted to Him. I'd truly believed God's perfect plan for my life was marriage to show God's love in that heavenly-ordained, though presently much-maligned and scrutinized sacrament. Certainly what ensued would verify my belief, for one-and-a-half years later, while living a richly satisfying single life, I met Rand. We met in church, and I can honestly say I struggled against any relationship with him except friendship. Initially

I wouldn't even entertain the thought that God would give me a third chance at marriage. That thought was absolutely incomprehensible. Though I firmly believe what Anne Graham Lotz says in *Just Give Me Jesus*—that our God is the God of the slim chance, the fat chance, the no chance, and the last chance, none of that personally pertained to me. Yet after months of prayer we came to understand God's intention for us, and after almost two years together we quietly committed our lives to one another and to God's purposes.

Today, despite some ongoing challenges in our health and extended families, challenges similar to everyone else's, we are enjoying a sweet oneness and fruitfulness. Our relational dynamic is easygoing, and finally I'm wholly free to be myself—to share my opinions without my husband seeing them as challenges. Rand values what I "bring to the table" and loves me to laugh. When I sometimes revert back to extreme quietness—a self-protective behavior I'd developed over the years—he gently leads me out of myself to talk about the issues at hand. He'll have none of my old "stuffing" feelings. He's healthy and confident enough in himself and our commitment to each other to draw me out, though he may not always initially like my "take" on a matter. He's gracious that way, so I feel "safe" emotionally for the first time in my life. And because of the place I'm in today, I can see what a marvelous God we're privileged to serve, who would continue to work in our lives, giving us endless chances to fulfill His will—despite our failures, disappointments, and sorrows.

While I gave up on my dreams long ago, God never gave up on them and has worked quietly and steadily, oftimes unknowingly to me, behind the scenes, to bring about the plans He had for me from the very foundations of time. One of my deepest and most sincere prayers is that, having been given a third chance at marriage, Rand and I can show to others the blessing marriage is designed to be, both for the wedded two and also for those they are privileged to touch and influence. For has God not said "Two are better than one for when one falls down the other can help him up; it is not good that man should live alone?" (Ecclesiastes 4:9, 10 KJV and Genesis 2:18 KJV) In closing my story, I want to share that I see now my heart's desires really were His, not just mine, all along, and though it took three chances, He continued working with me until they were accomplished.

It Makes No Never Mind

This much I know . . . Our God is steadfast.

. . . "For He is the living God and he endures forever; his kingdom will not be destroyed; his dominion will never end."
—Daniel 6:26 NIV

He is ever focused on me in love; I have engraved you on the palms of my hands: your walls are ever before me.
—Isaiah 49:16 NIV

The dictionary defines *steadfast* as "firmly fixed, constant and unchanging, directed fixedly toward one point." I've come to know and love this characteristic of God above all others. I guess a person's favorite Bible verse often reflects his life's particular challenges and the roads he's traveled; at least it's so with me.

My story really begins with my search for truth during my college years. That search ended in a little country church where I accepted Jesus Christ as my personal savior, and almighty God as my Abba Father.

After completing my formal education, I met Hal, who back then had a vibrant faith and desire to seek and follow the Lord. After marriage, we were youth leaders together for a while in a small but sweet suburban church. All seemed well for a good while, so God's steadfast character was yet to be especially meaningful to me. But several more years into the marriage, Hal began to walk away from the Lord and began displaying a pattern of worldliness and deception. Nothing I could say or do would change his mind—really it was a heart problem; his heart had turned cold. He would do his thing, regardless of the hurt to me or our three children. Then came the night that I received the dreaded phone call from "the other woman." As the marriage had been sliding downhill for a while by his choice and behavior, I had begun increasingly, desperately clinging to the Lord, always finding Him there for me, a sure friend, a place of refuge. So when the inevitable call came that fateful night, the Lord was steadfast. He provided for me a wise pastor, who counseled that I wait for the right time to confront Hal. Also the Lord, in time, gave me both grace and strength to let Hal go, though I still loved him deeply, when after a two-year separation he asked for a divorce. But I've found the Lord even more steadfast after Hal and I remarried several years later.

For though Hal returned to the Lord to some degree, the years since have borne out the truth that he never again had the same hunger and sincere relationship with God he'd had as a young adult. Instead, and in spite of words to the contrary, he is generally disinterested in Christian activities, fellowship, and Bible reading. He is lukewarm at best, and that has had a great negative effect on all of us. Still we have stayed together despite our differences. I have found the Lord to be a constant, unchanging companion, helping me continue to be faithfully devoted to Hal, regardless of the passing circumstances or my fleeting and fluctuating feelings.

Dietrich von Bonhoeffer is one of my Christian mentors — a great man of faith living in Germany in the twentieth century. I see and would emulate his faithfulness to the Lord, regardless of being sentenced to death unless he recanted what he knew and professed to be absolute truth concerning our faith and Jesus. He chose death rather than reject the Lord, and I garner strength from his example, desiring to be "firmly fixed" to the end also.

With three grown children now I still face issues, as Hal refuses to stand up for truth as the Bible presents it — unwavering, clear and a plumb line, by which to measure our lives and guide our steps. The result is I'm often characterized by the kids as the "Bible thumper" when I simply contend for a truth that in today's society is twisted or maligned. Still when I experience and remember the Lord's steadfastness in His earthly life (especially in embracing the cross) and its manifestation to me personally in everyday situations, I take heart and can stay the course, standing alone and knowing one day I'll be glad. "It makes no never mind," as the saying goes, whether I am happy today. Happiness isn't my goal, pleasing God is. And, I have a deep-seated unshakable confidence in the future, plus a settled peace about my present life.

No matter what happens this side of eternity, I know I'm not alone and will never be alone, forgotten, or unloved. I'm looking forward with a settled assurance to the day when my faith turns to sight. As the old hymn writer put it, "one day it will be worth it all" (*When we See Christ* by Esther Kerr Rusthoi) and for me this is the only hell I'll ever know, for heaven awaits me. Meanwhile I just keep my hand in the hand of my steadfast God and can say honestly, that is enough.

New Country

This much I know . . . Our God is worthy of sacrifice.

By faith Moses, when he had grown up, refused to be known as the son of Pharaoh's daughter. He chose to be mistreated along with the people of God rather than to enjoy pleasures of sin for a short time. He regarded disgrace for the sake of Christ as of greater value than the treasures of Egypt, because he was looking ahead to his reward . . . he persevered because he saw him who is invisible.
—Hebrews 11:24-27 NIV

I grew up in China, where ancestral worship and Buddhism were the state religions, but my family was Christian and the church was our life. My father, when a young unconverted adult, held a high position in the government until he sensed the emptiness of "high places" and, through the influence of strong believers, received Christ as Lord. Following this decision, he began holding gospel meetings to share his newfound faith, behavior that quickly landed him in prison. Having served his time, at his release he worked in a Christian bookstore until we all emigrated to the U.S. a few years later.

In our home church in Taiwan, because Christianity was not the state religion, though it was nominally tolerated, we were taught and nourished from our initial conversion "to count the cost." Persecution, hardship, and separation from family often followed a new believer's announcement of reception of Christ. Therefore one did not become a Christian casually. For us salvation was not a ticket into heaven so much as the beginning of a new life lived solely for the one true God, Jesus Christ. From the beginning it was not an "add-on" to life, but its true meaning and source. Nothing for us was sugar-coated, and from day one we understood and accepted Jesus as Lord, not just savior. Further, we were given to understand that our salvation is primarily for God's, not our own, sake, and our lives after the second birth are to be lived for the welfare of the body of Christ. The emphasis in our schooling over the years was to be for His glory. You do whatever is needed to fulfill His will. This is taught as "the glorious life." This is honor. Neither do we consider it sacrifice. It is simply life in Christ. After what He did for us on the cross, He deserves our doing whatever He asks. We are His soldiers, His army, and His witnesses. We further are taught that having been chosen by Him for His purposes, He will prepare us to speak for Him. This is our destiny, and we embrace it wholeheartedly.

A life-defining moment happened for me at Sunday school when I was quite young. They told us a story that became written on my very heart. During an earlier day of Christianity when believers were sacrificed for their faith, a certain young woman was being marched in a line into the Roman Coliseum to be thrown to the lions. To give her one last chance to renounce the faith, her children were brought to her side. Upon seeing them, she did the only thing she could. She broke ranks with the others in line and ran as fast as she could towards the lions. And so we were taught the true worth of our Lord and were given to understand that our lives were to be used in service and surrender to Him and His kingdom's cause, whatever the personal loss. Our culture itself taught that self came only after family honor. Family was the greater thing, self the lesser. Likewise we learned also, as children, to have eternity as our goal. Personal self-fulfillment was never an issue, let alone life's focus as it oftentimes is in the western world.

A second story that impacted me powerfully was that of another young woman taken to a city square and required to stand on a platform all day. Her crime: not giving up her Bible to the authorities who required it. Instead she clutched it to her heart as she stood before the people, until at the end of the day she was forcibly lain down and arms stretched out. The officials proceeded to smash her hands with a lead pipe until the Bible fell to the ground. This was done as an example to other believers. Yet in a later time when a missionary came to her village offering free Bibles, with her arms now stumps, she nonetheless joyfully reached out for a Bible to call her own once again—so great was her love of God's Word.

Having these stories and truths deeply embedded in my heart as a child made moving to America a pure joy. I thought here in a Christian country I would find a freedom to worship and serve the Lord not available back home, and people everywhere happily traveling the same road. But I had a rude awakening—especially in myself. I found instead that the freedom permitted here seemed to contribute to a people lost in their "liberty in Christ"—a people sold out to the American dream of pursuing the good life, as defined by each individual and the media. I found myself, having finished my formal education at the university, now married with children, a lovely home, dear husband, and good job, strangely distanced from the Lord, and dissatisfied with my obtainments.

I found and still find myself yearning for the days back home, when Christ was my all in all. For truly only He and His purposes can fulfill the heart's deepest need. I've slipped into the American mindset that does the lazy, self-centered thing. To be honest, it has become an effort these days even to discipline myself to have quiet time with the Lord alone, after the demands of a busy workday. But at least I am now recognizing this problem simply as sin—this refusal to make Jesus the priority in my life, and to be "sold out" to Him. And I am taking some steps to change, because it troubles me deeply that the good things I have and the good life He's given me I allow to rob me of the higher calling—loving and serving Him. The example of my father's life and suffering, which was so purifying and directional for me as a youngster, is sadly not the example I am presenting to my children.

I am thankful for my heritage and the truths learned at my father's knee. As they continue to call me back to a deeper dedication to the Lord, I also am challenged by the lives of others, such as my brother, living in Dallas, Texas. His church is involved in campus ministry in a town about a half hour from the city itself. For this ministry's purpose, church leaders asked that several people sell their homes and move to the immediate university area to be available "on site" 24/7 for any students' needs, in their outreach to them. My brother and his family answered the call with no thought to the personal loss or cost. Now students have access to his home whenever and for as long as they need it. His life is being spent for the body, which Christ loves. This, as I said before, is my present challenge as well, to return to the place I once was—sold out and seeking first, second, and third His kingdom. For truly I AM convinced, even if not living wholly this way, that our God is worthy of any and every sacrifice. A life lived any other way is really wasted.

Forty-Two Years Later

This much I know . . . Our God is faithful . . . especially to the living in death

For thy Maker is thine husband . . .
—Isaiah 54:5 KJV

I was fifteen when I first met Ned. We dated for five years, when I shared with him that I wanted a husband who would attend church and care about the Lord as well as for me and any children we might have. He agreed, so at age twenty we married. That was more than fifty years ago.

Typical of our generation, we had a traditional style marriage. I managed the home and Ned was the financial provider. While we discussed issues and problems together, he made the final decisions concerning them and us. He was efficient and organized, and I well cared for. As time passed we had four children, raised them to adulthood, and were very happy for forty-two years. I knew I was truly blessed and even today sometimes stop to thank God for the man He gave me to in marriage. Moving to that last year we spent together, Ned had several health problems. Some were heart-related, as he'd previously had bypass surgery. He was on medication for fibromyalgia and colitis. Perhaps that's why I wasn't too surprised the night I overheard him telling a dinner guest that when his "time came" he wanted to go quickly. But we never spoke of it ourselves. And despite his health issues, our daily routine was normal for retirees, so when he insisted on accompanying me to our daughter's home for a week one February to help with a new baby, all appeared well.

On the seventh morning, the day we were to return home, our daughter asked me to help set up an area downstairs for changing the baby. This involved stocking up on clothes and certain baby supplies. We decided to drive to a nearby department store to make the necessary purchases and took with us the three older grandchildren. As we began our little trip a light snow started to fall, but we proceeded anyway. Shortly thereafter a mail truck exiting a driveway appeared out of nowhere, blocking our way. Ned swerved to avoid hitting it. Our car then slid into the opposite lane, where we were hit broadside. At impact I turned to check the children in the back seat and noted they were okay, had only small cuts. Then I turned to Ned, asking him if he were alright. He said yes, but I gave him a nitroglycerin tablet anyway. He put his head back against the car seat rest and in less than a minute was gone. I knew it, understood it instinctively, but by God's grace alone had a calm presence of mind.

From that moment on I was to learn of God's faithfulness in an entirely new way. Heretofore I had seen it evidenced in ours and our children's lives in differing ways according to their needs, but now alone, a single again after forty-two years of marriage, God became my very real Husband. Bewildering challenges arose beginning that day, as I was one unprepared for widowhood, since I'd been cherished and kept. Though Ned had tried to teach me how to handle things like the checkbook, I'd not wanted to learn and had paid little attention to his instructions. Then, too, my widowed mother lived with us, so while I wasn't now alone in the house, that situation, being alone with her, was daunting. In the past our relationship had been strained sometimes, and Ned had been our buffer, extraordinarily kind to her. The loss of his presence changed our dynamic drastically. Now I was her sole caretaker, and the home itself, an older one with many large rooms, had its own issues. The roof leaked some and the heating system needed replacing. A gargantuan problem was the computer—a complete stranger to me, which had all our personal and financial data; and I couldn't even access the records, let alone understand or manage them.

Providentially, I'd grown in my relationship with the Lord over the years to the point I did spend time alone with Him each day in prayer and Bible reading. How fortunate I was that I learned to be disciplined in this way, for now I was utterly dependent upon Him for guidance. While I knew Ned as a believer was well and happy in heaven, and that knowledge gave me great peace on one hand, on the other I was left here on earth to adjust to his physical absence. I desperately missed our long talks, deep communications, and just having a companion with whom to do things, someone with whom to share everything. But as I'd practiced God's presence more and more, literally talking to Him when in the car, in the stores, or upon my bed, the loneliness that threatened to overtake me stayed at bay.

I knew I could call upon the children and other friends for advice and help, and sometimes did, but increasingly I came to call upon the Lord as I once had Ned, in a husbandly capacity, and found strength and answers to my questions coming directly from Him.

One huge confusing area He led me through was the insurance minefield. It was a real quagmire. I didn't know what I was entitled to or where to go for the best coverage. In the midst of the confusion I would often say, "Lord you can do this. Give me wisdom. Show me what to do"; and I stood on the promise in the Psalms that says, "I will instruct you, teach you in the way you should go. I will guide you with my eye" (Psalm 32:8 KJV). I'd reply "I'm counting on you Lord." Despite the prevailing wisdom not to make a big decision for one year after a spouse's death, I knew it was time to sell our home of twenty-five years. When the sale was accomplished, I prayed for specific guidance for a new place to live and looked at condominium complexes in six different towns. From all the possibilities I eventually chose one, and can say today, years later, there couldn't be a better fit. Its design, location, and residents all meet my particular needs. Truly God manifested His presence in leading me here.

A dear friend, relative actually, came alongside early on to walk me through the computer thing, so now I am able to function reasonably productively in that area also.

A very special example of God's husbandly love and care for me came when, for the first time, I went back alone to our timeshare. We'd always delighted in New England's fall beauty, and often while away, we'd use the timeshare as a place in which to just relax and do craft projects, while alternately enjoying nature's wonders. We truly had been given the ability to enjoy simple quiet tasks and joys together. Returning alone to the quietness could have been awful. Yet alone I went. Then one evening, surprisingly, for I'd purposed beforehand not to go there, I found myself in the resort's dining room. Where we'd once sat together, I now sat alone. Yet in an inexplicable way, I sensed Ned's overwhelming presence across the table. The moment wasn't difficult at all, but instead both comforting and sweet. I know the Lord gave me that "gift" to not only show me His love, but also to enable me to be unafraid to continue living freely, fully. Much as Ned himself had protected and provided for me, the Lord now did the same.

Early in my widowhood, I thought it would be wonderful to have a male friend one day—just to bounce things off and to do things with, but now after several years of being God's alone, I am content. I've learned experientially that He is faithfulness itself (a true husband to the husbandless) and all I'll ever need in companion and guide. His Word today is my deepest joy, and He Himself my portion. His presence is an abiding reality, and I'm sure will continue to be as the seasons and years pass. How blessed I am to have had two wonderful husbands—the first an earthly one made of flesh, the second a heavenly one of the spirit, but every bit as real. This much I know and can say—if you're facing the prospect of widowhood, you needn't be afraid—for He Himself as your Maker has promised to be your Husband, just as He is mine. And since He is God, He cannot lie, and He cannot fail.

Family, the First Thing

This much I know . . . Our God is faithful through the generations.

Tell ye your children of it, and . . . their children another generation.
—Joel 1:3 KJV

Just as none lives solely unto himself, and as each of us is to a large degree the product of both his ancestry and upbringing, so am I and my story primarily one of the importance of and love for family. My father never knew his own dad, and his mother was a part of his life only in its very early years. He was orphaned at age three, but then adopted by an aunt and uncle. My mother's mother, on the other hand, was widowed early in her marriage and blinded from young womanhood as well, so she lived most of her adult life with my mom, who cared for her for more than forty years. Ironically, my mom, like her mother, was widowed by age forty-one when my dad died unexpectedly while in recovery after shoulder surgery, so out of necessity and because it was the way things were done back then, the generations came to live together under one roof. I, then as a child, became part of what is known as "extended family living." The whole clan, all thirty-five of my cousins, aunts, and uncles, spent every Sunday afternoon together, sharing dinner, fellowship, and then a grand sort of amusement activity, by which we entertained one another with our varying talents. Once a summer, all of us, in- and out-of-state family members, gathered for a picnic/reunion at a state or local park. It is fair to say that in our family the generations lived and loved together, caring for and accepting each member from the eldest to the least, all inclusive. This then was the framework in which I viewed family. I saw it, above all else, as intergenerational.

I grew up to marry a man different in this respect. One in a family of eight children, because of long-standing alcohol problems, Les experienced his parents' great turmoil and dysfunction, ending in divorce, which severed the family's closeness. It didn't help that his family style was more like parallel play than engaged activity. By this I mean, though they did some things together, basically they functioned in work side-by-side, as opposed to "entering in" emotionally and intimately interacting with one another. It was just a different way of living from ours . . . but the differences only heightened my resolve to live as closely interconnected with all my family as possible.

In short order, after marriage our four children arrived, and life revolved around the home and them. But there came a day when our personal differences due to divergent upbringings converged to overwhelm us with huge problems. I shared my deep unhappiness with my brother and sister-in-law, who explained the real need in my life was a personal relationship with Jesus Christ, who was more than capable as God to meet those needs. After a period of time, sharing, and the further influence of other Christians, and out of sheer misery and desperation, I did as they all recommended, inviting Jesus into my life as Lord and Savior.

I was fortunate that early on the Lord brought many mature believers into my life to counsel me concerning my newfound salvation and its behavioral consequences concerning Les. He was a bit of a rascal, a skeptic, and not at all inclined to accept Jesus as Lord of his life. So I learned to walk carefully before him, with a quiet spirit. It was a year and a half before I first saw the Lord's faithfulness in bringing one of my family members to Himself, but at that time Les saw "the light" also. God's timing is so perfect. As I look back now, I can't imagine how we'd have weathered the storms of those next few years without being together in the Lord and am so glad that very quickly after experiencing salvation we became committed to a local church, found our spiritual gifts, and began serving others even as they began serving us.

An area of great testing for us in the Lord's faithfulness in the family was about to come in our kids' teenage years. Even before becoming a believer, morals had been a big issue for me, so it was terribly troubling to have two of the children make poor moral choices with huge long-range implications. Yet in the midst of the challenges, we learned not to write the kids off but to practice unconditional love for them, hating the sin but loving the sinner. Their poor choices, though, turned out to be exactly the tools God used to draw them to Himself. By their late twenties, all four had professed Jesus and evidenced His salvation to widely varying degrees.

Shortly after this point in time a crisis hit my mom-in-law. Early on, our relationship had been rough. Because she had resented Les' becoming engaged so young, my feelings toward her were mixed from the get-go. Still I'd honored her, calling her "mom," and showing her every respect that position requires. Now she had outlived three husbands and fallen upon financial hard times in her retirement years, having no way to pay the rent and stay in her apartment alone. We opened our home to her, first on weekends, and later fulltime. She came to us with special physical needs, as she was just recovering from a stroke, and shortly thereafter needed a leg amputation because of arterial sclerosis. We became her primary caregivers. At one point because I worked fulltime, the sisters in the church took two to three hours shifts caring for her and provided a fresh casserole every night for months. The bigger miracles though were the softening of our hearts, mine so as to come to love her deeply, and hers so as to come to love and receive Jesus.

Next in the blessings to the generations, the Lord allowed me the privilege of leading my five grandchildren, my own mother, and an uncle all to the Lord. Two sons-in-law and a daughter-in-law also "professed" Christ, and so the chain goes on.

As I pray now often for the remaining members of my extended family, I am confident that the great God, who loves all and wishes for me to have my earthly family complete in heaven, will continue to be faithful. With His promise to me, I generally rest peacefully, awaiting its fulfillment. Because my God is the generational God of Abraham, Isaac, and Jacob, and desires with all His heart that families in eternity be found complete in Him, I trust Him with the future necessary work in my loved ones lives to that promised end.

The Gift of His Choosing

> This much I know . . . Our God is a God who gives first, not second best, if we leave the choice to Him.
>
> . . . Whatever things ye desire, when ye pray, believe that ye receive them, and ye shall have them.
> —Mark 11:24 KJV

God does all things by design, not willy-nilly, as we humans sometimes do. And, the fullness of time bears out His wisdom and kindness to us in His choices. I surely saw this truth at work a couple years ago, when my husband had the opportunity "to plant a church," thereby fulfilling a cherished dream, in a town about ninety miles from our first home.

There came the day when we believed it was time for Caleb to leave his present job and seek the position he'd been awaiting. Throughout this time of praying and expectation, like many young women, I began to envision our new home, for the new job would surely require a move. I liked our present home, a small cape cod, but in truth we had outgrown it, and found it limiting when entertaining guests. It was in that timeframe that my husband awakened me one morning to tell me of a dream he'd had. This alone was interesting, as he hardly ever recalled having had a dream. He shared that he'd seen a home with lots of dark wood and stone. I was excited; I imagined something stately, refined, a thing of beauty.

The new job offer came, but with it an unexpected blow. The financial package came in much lower than we had anticipated, so this would be a lateral move at best. I struggled with this information particularly since the new area we'd live in was one of nation's "hot real estate boom" areas, where home prices had soared through the roofs. So clearly this move would be a backward one financially. Yet we knew the job opportunity had his name all over it, so we clung to the scriptural belief that God who loves us, understands us and our needs, would withhold from us no good thing. But I had to choose to actively believe that, as we sought first the Lord's work and kingdom, the "other" things would be added unto us as well.

The job offer having been accepted, the search for a new home began in earnest. Working fulltime, we were limited by time constraints in looking at places in the new town, two hours away. Also limiting was the fact that, because our new area was "hot," homes stayed on market only a day or two, sometimes selling even mere hours after being listed.

A strange thing happened as we began our search. Driving home one morning, gazing out the car window at various houses, a thought popped into my head that I should be willing to look at a "tri-level," a type of home I don't particularly care for. The thought was more relevant than I could ever have known then.

Our search began without finding anything to our liking in our price range. We considered building, but couldn't find a location, plans, or builder that we liked. Next the realtor sent us a sheet of homes presently on the market. Our choices were bleak, and I became discouraged. I thought about renting, in hopes of something developing in the future, but Caleb didn't want to throw money away, as he perceived renting to be. Some time elapsed, and we began to feel squeezed, pressured. Then on the MLS listing one day, an older home in our price range popped up. It had potential, but frankly the potential could have been easily missed, given all the work the home needed. The yard was unkempt and the exterior ugly. But those paled in comparison to the inside. It looked like a cyclone had hit it, junk and food everywhere—darkness, distress, and neglect obvious to the most casual observer. I walked through the home quickly, trying to envision it renovated, after all it was big and did have brick and lots of dark wood (too much dark wood!). My heart sank, for somehow I knew this was "our house," and I wasn't at all sure I wanted it to be. My husband on the other hand, with great vision, was enthralled and wanted to bid on it immediately. I decided to call my mom—to use her as a sounding board. She was not surprised by my call, as that very morning she'd been led to fast and pray for the Lord to lead us to His choice of a home for us.

Things moved quickly after this. We put in a bid, only to receive, over the weekend, a call from a builder about a new property site that was coming available. Clearly, swiftly, what peace I'd had vanished, and Caleb and I were at odds. I saw new, modern, not this handyman's special we were bidding on. I could only imagine it being a money pit, and so we withdrew our former offer. Yet now, strangely, I had no peace at all, and Caleb's deep disappointment smote my heart. So I did the only thing I knew to do. I opened my Bible to read and I prayed. Within a couple minutes, a calm settled over me and the decision that just a few moments ago had seemed larger than life was no longer overwhelming. I knew that in resubmitting the offer that I would be honoring Caleb, so we did just that.

Our old home sold just two days before the contract on the new home would have lapsed and the owners accept a second back-up bid, that one not ours, of course. Still, at the closing of the new house, I half jokingly asked the lawyer if I really had to buy "this bundle of sticks." I had a peace, but no joy about the deal. I hadn't really accepted the fact—its present reality confronted my dream house so rudely. Oh those expectations! For weeks following, my husband, friends, and family toiled late into the morning's early hours, working to transform my bundle of sticks. Floors were ripped up, walls and ceilings painted, bathrooms gutted, and new appliances and counters purchased. Slowly the house was made new.

We moved in and made ready to begin to entertain, and I was amazed. It was as if the house had been built for that very purpose. Two dozen children can (and have) played in the family room downstairs while two dozen adults meet comfortably upstairs in the living room. The kitchen and dining rooms are large enough to feed several families at the same time. The large deck and backyard, with its poplar, hickory, and elm trees is park-like, the perfect setting for cookouts. With four bedrooms, family and friends can come to visit and sleep comfortably. As I recognized all these good features, it was then I remembered the list I had made of my dream house many months earlier. I had asked for a paved driveway, a nice piece of property, a home large enough for entertaining, with bright light (the house has large windows and two skylights), and fairly new construction (which it sort of has after its remake). I smiled as I looked at the list. God had led us to my dream house without my even knowing it. And to think I almost missed it because it wasn't in some ways what I'd had in mind. How fortunate we believers are that God always gives us His best when we leave the choice to Him.

Together by His Design

This much I know . . . Our God uses all things both great and small to work together to accomplish His purposes in His children's lives.

I have raised him up in righteousness, and I will direct all his ways . . .
—Isaiah 45:13 KJV

Mine is a love story, detailing the Lord's plan to bring me to Kent that we might partner together for Him all the days of our lives. It began eighteen years ago when Claire, a lady in my childhood church, developed a longing to see Martha's Vineyard. Perhaps she did this because she read of the place in mystery novels, and it piqued her curiosity, but the why is really insignificant. What is significant is that her desire was born in the time period someone in her extended family owned a place in Orleans, Massachusetts, and she spent runaway weekends each year at their family cottage. At one such time, she and her family actually set out one morning to the Woods Hole Ferry for a day's outing on the Vineyard, but made the mistake of ferrying instead to Nantucket. She said later that though they had a beautiful day sight-seeing, shopping, and "mopeding" on the island's cobblestone streets and quaint pathways, she came away inexplicably dissatisfied, desiring all the more to see the Vineyard. Over the next several years, from time to time, she'd ask her husband if they might not tour it, but for no particular reason he'd deny her wish. She always accepted his refusal with a quiet grace, believing that in the fullness of time the joy she anticipated would be hers.

Fifteen years passed until a friend of theirs inherited part ownership in the only timeshare on Martha's Vineyard and asked Claire if they'd like to visit overnight. Plans were made, but were almost amended when a health issue popped up mysteriously the day of the trip. But determinedly, Claire pressed through, and she and her husband drove to Cape Cod as planned, with a new stop-off thrown in. A friend of hers, whose son had a house in the area, also was vacationing up there at the time and invited them to stop by for coffee. While there, at the friend's home, Claire "chanced" to speak briefly with the younger son of her hostess. She had not seen the young man in years, and that he was there at all at that time was both unexpected and most interesting, as it was his older brother Claire had been told she'd see. But as with all the paths God leads His children down, this was no chance encounter, but instead a life-defining moment. Claire now shares, "When I looked into his eyes, I saw a young woman, and sensed God at work."

Returning from the weekend jaunt three days later, she called my mom to see whether I was "involved" in a dating relationship. I wasn't, but was slated to be out of the states for the summer on a South American mission trip, pursuing God's direction for my future. I returned stateside in late August, and by October, Kent and I were emailing, despite my apathy. I had so much going on in my life at that time—right after college graduation—new friends, first job, first car, first apartment, and the prerequisite adjustments encumbered with all of them. Nevertheless, email we did and in December had our first date. We were engaged in February and married the following October.

But there's a second side to our story that shows God's work in His children's lives is thorough and perfectly timed, though generally hidden till He reveals it. Kent had been struggling in that very timeframe with whether he would marry at all or instead live celibate, simply for the Lord alone. Only a month before we began emailing, he'd admitted that he was content to live single all of his days, yielding his former desire for marriage—now surrendering total control his life to the Lord. In doing so he could not have guessed he was positioning himself to be led to me.

Simple as our story is, I find in it a great truth about God, namely that He is in the starts and stops of our lives and will not fail over time to bring about His plans for us, IF we desire He do so. Interestingly, Claire has subsequently marveled that had she seen Martha's Vineyard any other time over the years prior to when she did, one visit would have been enough. For despite the many years longing, and not being disappointed by its rugged beauty and charm, the two day tour of the island would have been sufficient for them. They'd not have returned again, but turned their sights to a different tourist spot. Most certainly they'd not have been on the cape that providential day they visited Kent's mom for a cup of coffee, a house tour, and a prophetic moment of understanding that would forever define my life.